"I read Florence's books with a smile on my face because I love her humor and writing style. I also read with pen and paper in hand because I gain so much insight that can be applied to my pastoral and speaking ministries. Florence is not only one of my favorite authors, she is also an outstanding communicator."

John Maxwell, Author
Pastor, Skyline Wesleyan Church

"As I have traveled throughout the United States and Canada I continually hear great comments about Florence and her ministry. She is on the cutting edge of women's needs. Her ministry, through books and in person, stimulates lasting growth in many, including myself."

Joanne Wallace, Author
President, Image Improvement, Inc.

"You are truly a gifted writer, Florence! Thank you for creating another masterpiece. Your writing has touched so many lives, and I know that through this book you will continue to be a blessing."

Sylvia Nash, Executive Director/CEO
Christian Ministries Management Association

"Thank you again for being an extraordinary role model. Your professionalism, dedication and talent give much glory to the Giver of gifts!"

Liz Curtis Higgs, Professional Speaker
National Speakers Association Member

"Florence Littauer is an absolute genius. She is a real pioneer, helping the Christian world face and deal with issues we have wanted to deny. Her writing leads all of us to become more honest and more truly Christian."

Jan Ream, Author
Co-founder, New Source Counseling Centers

Also available from Here's Life Publishers —

Freeing Your Mind
From Memories That Bind
by Fred and Florence Littauer

THE BEST OF

Florence Littauer

Compiled by

Marilyn Willett Heavilin

Here's Life Publishers

First printing, June 1989

Published by
HERE'S LIFE PUBLISHERS, INC.
P. O. Box 1576
San Bernardino, CA 92402

Library of Congress Cataloging-in-Publication Data
Littauer, Florence, 1928-
    The best of Florence Littauer: on understanding yourself and the people
around you / compiled by Marilyn Willett Heavilin.
    p.   cm.
    Includes index.
    ISBN 0-89840-260-3
    1. Christian life—1960-   . 2. Personality—Religious
aspects—Christianity.   3. Interpersonal relations—Religious
aspects—Christianity.   I. Heavilin, Marilyn Willett.   II. Title.
BV4501.2.L547   1989   89-32078
248—dc20   CIP

For More Information, Write:
L.I.F.E.—P.O. Box A399, Sydney South 2000, Australia
Campus Crusade for Christ of Canada—Box 300, Vancouver, B.C., V6C 2X3, Canada
Campus Crusade for Christ—Pearl Assurance House, 4 Temple Row, Birmingham, B2 5HG, England
Lay Institute for Evangelism—P.O. Box 8786, Auckland 3, New Zealand
Campus Crusade for Christ—P.O. Box 240, Colombo Court Post Office, Singapore 9117
Great Commission Movement of Nigeria—P.O. Box 500, Jos, Plateau State Nigeria, West Africa
Campus Crusade for Christ International—Arrowhead Springs, San Bernardino, CA 92414, U.S.A.

Special Thanks

We are grateful for the generous permission granted by those companies that originally published the material included in this volume. Our thanks goes to our good friends at Revell, Harvest House, Word, Here's Life, and Huntington House, who have given their full cooperation to the reproduction of these materials in the spirit of Christian fellowship and in a desire to see these works reach an ever-expanding readership.

After Every Wedding Comes a Marriage by Florence Littauer. Copyright © 1981 by Harvest House Publishers. Used by permission.

Blow Away the Black Clouds by Florence Littauer. Copyright © 1979, 1986 by Harvest House Publishers. Used by permission.

Freeing Your Mind from Memories That Bind by Fred and Florence Littauer. Copyright © 1988 by Fred and Florence Littuaer. Used by permission of Here's Life Publishers.

How to Get Along with Difficult People by Florence Littauer. Copyright © 1984 by Harvest House Publishers. Used by permission.

It Takes So Little to be Above Average by Florence Littauer. Copyright © 1983 by Harvest House Publishers. Used by permission.

Looking for God in All the Right Places by Florence Littauer. Copyright © 1987 by Florence Littauer. Used by permisison of Word Books.

Out of the Cabbage Patch by Florence Littauer. Copyright © 1984 by Harvest House Publishers. Used by permission.

Personalities in Power by Florence Littauer. Copyright © 1989 by Huntington House, Inc. Used by permission.

THE BEST OF FLORENCE LITTAUER

Key to Sources

Quotations are followed by letter codes with numbers that indicate the title of the work from which the extract is taken and the page number on which it appears. For example:

> *If you want to increase your mental ability, start with the past. Don't be too busy with the present to reflect on the lessons of the past. (ITS/65-66)*

The letters *ITS* indicate the quotation is taken from *It Takes So Little To Be Above Average* and the numbers 65-66 indicate the quotation is found on pages 65 and 66 of that work.

Below is a list of the letter codes used in this collection and the works to which they refer:

AEW   *After Every Wedding Comes a Marriage*

BBC   *Blow Away the Black Clouds*

FYM   *Freeing Your Mind From Memories That Bind*

GAD   *How to Get Along with Difficult People*

ITS   *It Takes So Little to be Above Average*

LFG   *Looking for God in All the Right Places*

OCP   *Out of the Cabbage Patch*

PPO   *Personalities in Power*

PPL   *Personality Plus*

RTC   *Raising the Curtain on Raising Children*

BOX   *Silver Boxes*

YPT   *Your Personality Tree*

Contents

W

To the Reader

I first met Florence Littauer in the late sixties when we both were staff members of Campus Crusade for Christ. We quickly discovered that we had each experienced the loss of two baby boys prior to coming to California. Although it was our grief that drew us to each other, it was our love for God and our families, and our mutual enjoyment of leadership and meeting new challenges that allowed our friendship to continue over the past twenty some years.

As a new Christian, Florence had an unquenchable thirst for God's Word, and her enthusiasm was contagious. Soon I was involved in helping her conduct a women's Bible study in her home which quickly grew to more than ninety women. A couples' evening Bible study developed from the women's group, and my husband Glen and I were leaders for several years.

I remember Florence's first messages on depression, marriage, children and temperaments. I was impressed then, and I am still impressed today. Florence has an ability to make the complex simple and to always make people feel hopeful that they and their situation can improve.

As a student at CLASS (Christian Leaders and Speakers Seminars) and as a CLASS staff member for the past three years, I have watched Florence encourage hundreds of men and women to discover their own temperaments, deal with the pains of the past and refine their skills to become the unique individuals God intended them to be rather than clones of Florence Littauer or anyone else.

THE BEST OF FLORENCE LITTAUER

Florence not only teaches others, but she also continues to learn—she will never be stagnant. Since 1978 she has written fifteen books, and I have had the privilege to help with the typing and editing on eight of those projects.

I am excited about *The Best of Florence Littauer,* and I see several ways it can be used. For those of you who are always looking for good material to use in your own speaking and writing, this book is for you! You'll find many quotable quotes on a variety of topics. Many of you will enjoy reminiscing as you read quotes and favorite stories from Florence's books you have already read. If you have never read a Florence Littauer book, use this volume to whet your appetite and help you decide which book to read first.

As you read, take time to appreciate Florence's use of alliteration, her wonderful ability to make everyday experiences come alive and her love for God. Florence desires most to help her readers become hungry to learn more about God and have an influence on their world.

Outside of God and my family, few people have had a greater influence on me than Florence. She helped me get excited about studying God's Word, comforted me after the death of my third son, gave me hope that God could use me to help other grieving people, gave me opportunities to speak and gently nudged me until I finally wrote my first book, *Roses in December.*

I am grateful for the opportunity to compile the material in *The Best of Florence Littauer* as a thank you to my friend and mentor.

Marilyn Willett Heavilin
Editor

Foreword

When I wrote my first book, *The Pursuit of Happiness,* I thought I had said everything I knew. I had told my life story from birth to the moment of writing. I had chronicled my childhood living in those now-famous three rooms behind my father's store in Haverhill, Massachusetts; my college years of physical, social and intellectual improvement; my wedding that was featured in LIFE magazine (May 18, 1953); my marriage problems which increased after the birth of two sons with fatal brain-damage; my depression over the hopelessness of my problems; my coming to the Lord Jesus for His healing touch; and the ministry and mission God quickly gave to Fred and me. When you have spelled out your life with its ups and downs, when you've been transparent about your strengths and weaknesses, what is there left to say?

Now, fifteen books later, I know there was much more to say. Branching off of the tragic circumstances of my two sons and my personal steps of recovery from depression, I found that people wanted to know how I'd recovered and how they could find peace. By the time I wrote *Blow Away the Black Clouds* I had been speaking and teaching on overcoming depression for eight years. I gave steps of self-help, counseling help and spiritual help. Recently I revised and updated the book. I added four new chapters including the subjects of teen depression and suicide, alternate types of counseling and the Christmas blues.

From the Harmony in the Home classes Fred and I taught in adult Sunday school, we wrote a course and began doing marriage seminars based on scriptural and practical suggestions for marital harmony. As the

17

demand for this information grew, I put it into a book—
After Every Wedding Comes A Marriage. In this book I
emphasized how the understanding of the four basic personality patterns had changed our marriage and helped
Fred and me see why we had never been able to accept
each other as we were and why we kept trying to transform each other.

This concept of discussing and discerning differences in personality became such a life-changing tool for so
many that I gathered humorous examples which people
shared with me and wrote *Personality Plus.* As this book
caught on, I began to do seminars on the subject of the
personalities. Little did I realize at the time of writing
Personality Plus that the concept of the temperaments
would be used of the Lord to change thousands of lives
and to put me in demand as a speaker across the country.
People loved the funny stories, the simplicity of the subject matter and the practicality of the principles.
Everyday became a new learning experience for me, and
each group of people provided me with a laboratory of ex-
perimentation.

Soon I could see every person and problem as an
example and as I grew in knowledge so did the scope of
my teaching. *How to Get Along with Difficult People*
placed the personalities into the church and showed how
to understand and deal with people like Joyce Judging,
Bob Bossy, Gloria Gossip and Debbie Depressed.

The more I studied the more I saw into the depth
of people's personalities, the emotional needs each type
has, and the effect parental control, rejection or abuse
has on the child's growth. I found that many people in
taking the Personality Profile had no idea who they were,
were scattered across the board or had opposing traits. I

had to find answers to why my mother-in-law, a dynamic Choleric, saw herself as a Phlegmatic. The outgrowth of this study on why people wear masks over their birth personality is the book *Your Personality Tree.* In this I trace our families back several generations and show others how to discover who they really were created to be.

In *Your Personality Tree* I have two chapters on the personality of parents and their children. Because of the popularity of these sections, I planned a book *Raising the Curtain on Raising Children* and showed in it how each type of parent relates to each child differently. I had been mentally writing this book for years but I waited until my youngest was twenty-five before I dared put on paper the plans, practices and prayers that produced successful adults out of our children. The response to the ideas in this book, the creative conversations, work charts, prayer cards, basic table manners and ways to make the home fun, has been most gratifying to me. One lady wrote, "Thanks for taking the time to teach me to teach my children what my mother had not taught me."

Beyond the individual and family application of the personalities, I began to use the concept in my leadership training to show that we can all be successful if we function in our natural strengths and work to overcome our weaknesses. For years I have been collecting stories on political figures and analyzing their personalities. I've shown in my seminars why Choleric Nixon thirsted for power, why Phlegmatic Ford rested in peace, why Melancholy Carter labored for perfection, and why Sanguine Reagan enjoyed popularity. Audiences loved the insight and the humor as I showed how each president came in on his strengths and went out on his weaknesses. People asked, "Do you have the presidents material in a book?" That question started a study of the personalities

from Franklin Roosevelt through George Bush, conclud-
ing in a review of the 1988 campaign. This became the
book *Personalities in Power: The Making of Great
Leaders.*

In the midst of my twenty years of immersion in
the personalities, I have written *Shades of Beauty* with
my daughter Marita and *Out of the Cabbage Patch.* The
latter grew from a message I gave spontaneously on the
reasons why the Cabbage Patch dolls caught on: They
were unique, one-of-a-kind; they were in need of a home;
and they were adoptable. I showed how we are all God's
Cabbage Patch dolls. We are unique, in need of a Savior
and adoptable into the family of God. I told the story of
my adopted son Fred, born of two people who should
never have gotten together in the first place. I shared
how he was in need of a home and he was adoptable.

When I gave this message to a group of teens they
got very quiet as I talked about my son, so I added the six
reasons why young people feel it's all right to fool around
starting with "It'll never happen to me" and ending with
"I can always give it up for adoption." I showed them the
fallacy in this kind of thinking and admonished them to
not leave little Cabbage Patch Dolls around the country
for people like me to adopt. The impact this message had
on adults and teens alike caused me to put it into a book.

Besides the topics of testimony, depression, marriage, personalities, child raising, politics, fashion and
teen morality, I have always loved the area of leadership
and at one point I was almost a professional president.
Putting together my years of civic and social leadership,
my Christian commitment and my desire to raise the
levels of Christian speaking, I founded CLASS (Christian
Leaders and Speakers Seminars) in 1980. Since that time

the Lord has raised up a staff of dedicated leaders from different backgrounds and with unique experiences to assist me in encouraging others to become speakers, teachers, leaders and writers. From the success of this program came not only the three-day seminar CLASS, but a workbook and cassette presentation titled *Say It with CLASS* and later the motivational book *It Takes So Little to be Above Average.*

One day my daughter Marita said to me, "You've been teaching Bible studies for years but you've never written a book showing how you make the study of the Scripture practical in everyday life. Why don't you do that next?" Because of my love for the Old Testament and my delight in applying truth to life, I began an exciting journey through Genesis and Exodus that became *Looking for God in All the Right Places.* For years women had asked, "Do you have any Bible study materials we can use in our group?" Because of this need I wrote the book with questions and assignments appropriate for class use or personal study. I loved the hours I spent meditating on God's Word and putting what He taught me into an explanation for others. Although it is not my best selling book, *Looking for God* will always be one of my favorites.

In the last five years as my schedule has increased and Fred has been traveling with me, we have seen a dramatic rise in the severity of people's problems which they bring to us for counsel. We have listened to tales of abuse, rape and incest, of alcohol, drugs and other addictive practices, of sexual perversions and damaged emotions. As the need for understanding, explanation and restoration became critical, Fred and I listened closely to the diversity of physical, spiritual and emotional pain and we prayed for insight and wisdom. The Lord brought individuals before us that had lived through and triumphed over an abundance of adversities.

We put on a HOPE conference (Helping Other People Emotionally) with fifteen women sharing their life experiences. Word Publishers recorded this seminar and produced a tape series to assist counselors, pastors and individuals in overcoming their own problems and providing hope for others. As Word worked on the cassette production, they asked me to write a book telling these stories. This became *Lives on the Mend,* recently retitled *Hope for Hurting Women.*

Soon we saw that people in pain needed more than the inspirational story of another to recover from a life-time of hurts. Because of a lack of knowledge, well-meaning friends and counselors had told victims: "Pray about it and it will go away"; "I'm sure he never did that to you. It's all in your mind"; "If you'd only forgive him, you'd feel much better"; or "If you were really a Christian, you wouldn't have this sin in your life in the first place."

As women, and sometimes men, told us their tragic tales, we knew we had to do something specific to help. One day in May 1988 as we drove away from a retreat of 800 women where we had counseled until two in the morning, we both felt as if we were deserting a sinking ship. What could we do? Neither of us had time to write another book and I was already in the midst of creating *Personalities in Power* and *Raising the Curtain on Raising Children.*

The urgency we felt compelled us to find time in the middle of our hectic schedule to write *Freeing Your Mind From Memories That Bind.* Fred planned the outline, assigned me what part I should write and began work on his first manuscript. As we wrote at separate times and places, we both knew we were doing what the Lord had commanded us to do to help His hurting body. We had no idea how the chapters would fit together or whether our two styles of writing would coordinate. Fred took the parts and put them together. I never even read what he had written before it was sent to the publisher. When the manuscript was presented to a Christian psychologist-editor, he answered with approval of the content and this comment, "Although there are two names on this book, it is obvious only one of them did the writing." If ever the hand of God was on anything we've written, it is this book.

Affirming this thought is the fact that the publisher sold 30,000 copies in the first six months and that the response has been overwhelming. People are writing, "Finally a book that doesn't just talk about the problems but one that gives answers." God has called Fred and me to a ministry of encouragement, of giving hope to those who are hurting.

By the time I had finished three books in 1988, I really didn't feel like starting another one. But during that year my message on "Silver Boxes, The Gift of Encouraging Words" had become so popular that people were asking me when I would have a book on it. Because the message challenged others to develop their own God-given talents, people poured up after my speaking engagements to tell me what they could have been if only someone had encouraged them. Others realized they had children or grandchildren who needed to be praised and uplifted in order to fulfill their potential. People decorated luncheon tables with silver boxes, gave me all sizes and shapes of silver boxes, and wrote me silver box letters full of examples. I had no choice but to sit down, read all the personal testimonies, and weave them into a book of encouragement, *Silver Boxes.*

Throughout these years of writing and teaching as the Lord has led me from subject to subject, from place to place, from person to person, my friend Marilyn Heavilin has been both an observer of my life and a participant in my programs. She has seen the hand of God on my life and has shared my enthusiasm for meeting the needs of the people. She has taught Bible studies with me and has responded to my motivation by becoming an author, speaker and CLASS staff member.

When she suggested a *Best of Florence Littauer* book, I was flattered and overwhelmed with the thought. I didn't have her vision for what she had in mind, but in seeing the finished product I am amazed at how much I've said on a variety of topics and at her ability to pull out and index brief messages of meaning from the million plus words I've put on paper in the last ten years.

No one but Marilyn could have compiled this collection, for she is a friend who has known me closely both socially and emotionally, we have shared mutual griefs and heartaches and we have helped each other grow spiritually. In addition to our personal relationship, Marilyn has read each of my books as they have come out and has listened to my teaching for over twenty years. She has traveled with me and she has seen what sentences the Lord has used to change the hearts of the people.

Thank you, Marilyn, for putting your multiple talents to work on producing *The Best of Florence Littauer.*

Florence Littauer

A

ABUSE

As God gives us the ability to shut down our physical senses when we are in the midst of excruciating circumstances, so He provides an emotional escape when the situation is more than we can bear. When a little child is violated beyond her ability to emotionally handle the abuse, God gives relief by drawing a curtain of reprieve over the mind. The facts are still there, stored in the file drawers of the brain along with one hundred trillion other possible items, but they are covered up for the moment waiting for the damaged child to grow up and mature enough to be able to take the abusive evidence out, put it on the table, look at it, feel the pain again, and begin a program of restoration. (FYM/17)

□   □   □

Because of the natural trust of a child for her parents and her love for her siblings, the violation of her body by a family member is devastating and causes her to say to herself, "I'll never trust anyone again." She becomes suspicious of others and considers herself to be of no worth: "If I were a good girl, he wouldn't have done this." Abuse at home means there's nowhere to run for protection. (FYM/51)

□   □   □

The victimizer is often a legalistic Christian holding others to the letter of the law and a moralist who looks down upon those who don't meet his standards. He often picks up current causes, especially if they are against something, and he is definitely opposed to any kind of counseling. He prides himself on being a family man, keeps his children bound quietly and closely to him and is against any family visitation program. He appears very protective of his flock and often doesn't allow them to go on church picnics, campouts, or overnights at a friend's house, "all for their own good." He carries a big Bible, has a ready supply of memorized verses, and says "Amen" loudly at any appropriate moment. When it's his word against a child's, he is programmed to win.

Underneath the religious facade is a lonely man, probably abused as a child, who has deep feelings of inadequacy and wants desperately to be in control of his life or at least someone else's. He is socially immature, unable to relate with others on a feeling level and incapable of discussing anything deeply meaningful with his wife. Their sexual relationship ranges from mechanical to nonexistent and he usually feels inadequate and unfulfilled. If anyone really got to know him, they would find a pitiful self-destructive shell of a man. (FYM/56)

□   □   □

One night at a CLASS banquet I went to different tables to ask what each woman remembered about her mother. I was writing *Raising the Curtain on Raising Children* and I wanted some examples of what people would instantly recall about their mothers. At one table, the first four women all said, "She didn't protect me as I thought she would." Each one volunteered that she had been sexually abused by her father and in each case the mother had turned away and done nothing.

The first thing to realize is that many of these mothers have been in some way victimized themselves. Therefore, the thought of sexual molestation is not so shocking as it would be to someone who has not been abused. The mother almost always comes out of a dysfunctional family where learning to deny reality was an essential part of life. To face the day-to-dreary-day existence of an alcoholic father, an often-drugged mother, a brutal brother, a promiscuous sister, or any similar combination, the individuals involved have unwillingly become experts in denial. They've made excuses for why father couldn't go to work or why mother forgot to show up at school for an appointment. Life has become a tragic and deceptive game. When a woman from such a background gets married, she invariably marries a man with the capacity to molest. If she senses her daughter is being "played with" by her husband, she tends to look the other way, hope it's not happening, and deny the possibility. (FYM/59)

□   □   □

No child is born with a desire to be abused. But each baby has a longing to be loved, and when this affection is not given naturally in a positive way the child will take whatever attention comes his way. When a little girl is left alone with a father who is a potential perpetrator she doesn't know at first that this stroking and caressing could possibly be wrong. He tells her she's special and she can sense that she is pleasing her daddy. As he becomes more daring, her pleasure may turn to pain and soon she develops a love-hate relationship with her father. She loves the pleasure and hates the pain. (FYM/63)

□   □   □

Frequently an abuse victim has difficulty in accepting that God loves her unconditionally because her father who said he loved her violated her body. If her earthly father (step-father, uncle, etc.) professed love and at the same time hurt her, how can she believe in a loving God? Our image of God usually ties in with our feelings about our fathers. (FYM/67-68)

□   □   □

For the typically dysfunctional victim, sex becomes a way of looking for love with all the wrong people. Without some intensive searching of her childhood memories to come up with the cause of the distorted life, a dedicated prayer and study program, and a feeling of forgiveness from the Lord, a victim is patterned for repeating problems. (FYM/68)

ADOPTION

When Fred [my adopted son] was twelve years old he said to me, "I'm sorry you had those problems with your boys, but if it hadn't been for that I wouldn't be your son today. I would have been born anyway and somebody would have had me, but it wouldn't be you and I might not even be a Christian today." (AEW/19)

□   □   □

There is such a desire in human nature to belong to somebody or some group who will give us some collective identity. Many people join churches not because of interest in spiritual things but because they feel a need to belong. All of us want to know we have a home. We want to know we have someone who will marry us and bury us. We want to be part of a greater family; we want to be adopted into the family of God even when we don't understand our own desires. (OCP/60)

□   □   □

We told our son he was adopted long before he understood what it meant. I shared that he was special and that God chose him for us over all the other little boys in the world. We loved him dearly, and his two sisters, having lost two brothers, absolutely doted on him. In retrospect, I can see no way we could have done much better with him to make him feel loved. Yet when he was in his teens and the realization of his origin hit him, he came into our bedroom late in the evening and said, "I have something to say to you two." He had always had a gentle spirit but that night there was a tension and anger that we had not heard before. "I am not your flesh and blood. I do not have your drive and ambition. I am not as fast and as smart as Marita and Lauren and I never will be. The sooner you two get that into your heads the better off we'll all be." (RTC/95)

□   □   □

In July 1987, my husband and I conducted a

29

cruise to Alaska. Among the group of thirty couples, there were six who were adoptive parents. We were surprised to find each other and we shared our experiences. We all agreed that our adoptive children had an above average need for affection and assurance that they were loved and accepted. These children did seem to manifest the emotional responses to rejection; they had at some point lashed out at us in unexplained anger. Adopting a child, we all concluded, was not as simple as taking in a precious little baby and helping him grow up.

The results for us have been positive and the rewards even beyond that of our girls. Because they were our flesh and blood, we expected them to be exceptional. Then we lost our two boys and learned that we were fallible human beings who produced imperfect sons. Beyond that, God gave us our beautiful adopted son and we marvel at how he has matured into a responsible adult and businessman. (RTC/97)

□   □   □

As adoptive parents, when we are aware of the emotional burdens our children carry, we owe it to them to be understanding, to talk openly, and to listen without becoming defensive. We should entertain the possibility of outside counseling where the child can more freely vent his feelings without fear of reprisal. (RTC/98)

ADULTERY

In the past we dear Christian ladies have tried to avoid considering the possibility of the OTHER WOMAN. While *Cosmopolitan* is constantly concerned with the coquette, we have assumed that if our husband passes the cup on Sunday, he will pass up the cutie on Monday. As we have buried our heads alternately in the sink and the Scriptures, we have believed that our stable, substantial mates would appreciate our devotion to housework and mothering, and not expect us spiritual women to be sex kittens as well. We figured if we got meals on the table and suits home from the cleaners, we were holding our own. Sisters, that's not enough anymore.

With the blatant acceptability of "afternoon delights," sexual siestas seem to be replacing the salami sandwich. While we expect our husbands to be above this kind of thing, it is possible that a man who is upright today may be lying down tomorrow. (AEW/141)

□   □   □

If there's something your husband wants you to do, he's probably mentioned it before. Were you listening? Were you willing? Ask your husband what he'd want if he could choose another woman, and then keep quiet while he tells you. Why not become the *other woman* yourself and eliminate the chance for competition? It's better to *be* the other woman today than to *see* her tomorrow. (AEW/144-145)

AFFLICTED

First Timothy 5:10 stated, "Relieve the afflicted." To make sure I understood the meaning clearly I looked in the dictionary. *Relieve* means "to free from pain or embarrassment." The *afflicted* are "those depressed with continued suffering, misfortune or calamity." If you and I are to *relieve* the afflicted we must try to ease their pain and not embarrass them. So many of the cases I was told about had relatives or friends who added guilt to their pain and often hurt or ridiculed them in front of others. If you and I are to relieve the *afflicted,* we must help anyone we know who is distressed or depressed and who is suffering the loss of a loved one, the misfortune of a divorce or the calamity of cancer. (ITS/158)

□   □   □

When our families found out our first son was brain-damaged, there was a quick inspection of each side to see if there had been problems like this in the past. Somehow it seemed important to pin blame on the opposite side, but it didn't help me much to be questioned about any ancestors who might have been "a little off." (ITS/162)

□   □   □

When my second son was still alive, I'd occasionally have a dear little lady come up to me after I spoke and say, "If you were really a Christian you'd have your son home with you where he belongs." Since many of us in crises have only the Lord Jesus to depend on, it is devastating to have someone question your Christian commitment. (ITS/158)

□   □   □

I've never met a divorced person who is proud of it or who found it an exhilarating experience. None of us want it or recommend it, but when it is an accomplished fact, our Christian duty is to relieve the afflicted not heap guilt on them or show them where they were to blame. (ITS/161)

□   □   □

The easiest reaction to trauma in others is to ignore it. That way you don't have to view something difficult to look at or get yourself involved in something difficult to handle. In crisis times more people choose the "ignore the problem" method than any other. If you look the other way, it may go away. And it may, but not because of you. I have talked to so many women who in times of trauma were virtually abandoned by their friends and church. No one wants to see the retarded child, no one wants to get involved in the divorce, no one knows what to do with a rape victim, and no one enjoys weepy widows or dying cancer patients. It's so much easier to look the other way. How do you feel when you're the victim? Like you've got leprosy? Like you've been abandoned? The traumas of life aren't popular. New babies and broken legs we can handle, but keep us from having to love the unlovable. (ITS/162)

"ALERT TO LIFE"

My father not only read the paper each day but he gave us children capsulized versions of the day's news before we went to school. As I look back on it, I'm sure much of our success was due to his keeping our minds alert to life. (ITS/70)

□   □   □

Another obvious way to fill up the emptiness in our minds is to read everything, everywhere, at all times. If you're in the doctor's office and his magazines are twelve years old, rejoice. You can see firsthand how people were thinking then and compare it with the present for better or for worse. (ITS/69)

□   □   □

Read the paper each day. I try to at least glance through the paper before I go out each day. Even if I am teaching a seminar at 9:00 A.M., I see what happened overnight before going. I turn on one of the morning news shows while dressing and have an overview of the world before I leave to speak. It takes so little *time* to be ABOVE AVERAGE. I find people amazed that I, the speaker, have read the paper when they, the audience, are still buttoning their blouses. (ITS/69)

□   □   □

As an experiment I took ten *Time* magazine covers with pictures of people sufficiently prominent and current to be known around the world. I held them up in front of the audience and had the women write down the name of each person. Upon correcting the papers, we found that the average member of these ABOVE AVERAGE groups had three out of ten right.

If we leaders don't know what's going on in the world, who does? (ITS/69)

34

ANNOUNCEMENTS

The "Four Commandments of Announcements":

1. Make it CLEAR

2. Make it POSITIVE

3. Make it BRIEF

4. Make it COMPLIMENTARY (ITS/116)

APOLOGIES

Admitting we're wrong is not a sign of weakness, but of strength. It takes a real man to say he's sorry. Fred and I were married fifteen years before he ever said he was sorry for anything, and the first time he verbalized this thought I was overcome. I couldn't believe that perfect Fred could admit he was wrong.

When he said "I'm sorry," I heard "I love you."

In a teen-age group we took a survey of the words they most wanted to hear from their fathers. The majority reported:

"I love you" and "I'm sorry."

Your family knows you're not perfect, so why try to keep an act and have them see through it? Humble yourself when you're wrong and say those favorite of words — "I'm sorry." (AEW/125)

APPEARANCE

I believe I should dress in such a way that if I run

into Fred anywhere with a business associate, he can proudly introduce me and say, "This is my wife." I've taught my daughters, "If you walk out the door looking any less than acceptable, go back and change." One day my daughter Lauren called me up and said, "Mother, I want to tell you there's something you taught me that stuck." Now that's encouraging because sometimes we spend twenty-five years in training and we're not sure they heard a word we said! "I just thought you would like to know that I started out the door this morning in cut-off jeans and an old T-shirt, with no make-up and my hair kind of straight. I was just going to run to the store for something and as I walked out the door I remembered your words, so I went back and changed." (AEW/74)

APPRECIATION

How about your partner? Do you make him feel that he is the most important person in life to you? So many men are in a period labeled "Midlife Crisis." They feel useless and worthless. They look around at a busy wife and children who ignore them, they sense their job is going nowhere, and they say, "Is this all there is to life?" We women can help prevent this devastation if we renew our goal of putting our husband first.

You men so often take your wives for granted. You don't realize how dull her life seems compared to the magazines touting the superwoman success. She gets no pay for laundry and dishes; she has no hope for advancement. Can you let her know you appreciate her efforts? Can you take the burden of the children off her at least once a week? Can you uplift her, encourage her, and help her? Can you make her feel special? (OCP/58-59)

ATTITUDE

Before we open our mouths, people can sense our attitude. If we are haughty, critical, or bored, it shows and when we try to hide our true feelings, people can tell we are phonies. When our inner attitude is one of loving concern, we don't have to hand out lollipops to communicate our generous spirit. (ITS/104)

B

BEARING

A leader must have a beautiful bearing, a look of confidence. Make sure before presenting yourself to the court you're put together in such a secure way that you have no doubts draining your demeanor. What happens when you've left home with a button missing from your left sleeve? All day you keep your left hand behind your back, and don't dare reach for the coffee. What if there's a run in your pantyhose but you're in a hurry and you hope no one will notice? All day you keep standing in corners with your leg against the wall and when you leave rooms you back out. How nervous will you be if you tie a string around a too long slip and hope the lace won't show? You'll keep looking for mirrors to check your hem and you'll have a few friends watching for the fall.

When we are insecure on how we're put together, we waste a whole mental track on worry. We can't have the bearing of a queen when we wonder if our subjects will notice:

We've lost our buttons,

We're running in the wrong direction, and

We're held together by string.

For a regal radiance set your royal train on the right track. (ITS/108)

□   □   □

People love royalty. They want to look up to someone. They want an example to follow. When Jimmy Carter went into office, he misread the American public and thought they wanted a leader who was "one of the gang." He emphasized the ordinary, surrounded himself with down-home buddies and carried his own luggage. Surely there's nothing wrong with doing any of these things, but somehow he didn't come across as presidential. A flurry of articles came out on the qualities of a leader and we all began to ask ourselves what it was we wanted in a president. When given a new choice, we voted for an actor who had practiced for the presidential role and who surely looked the part. When President Reagan was asked a question on a TV press conference, he stood up straight, gave a confident smile, and said, "I'm glad you asked that question." He may not have known the answer, but he knew his ABCs of leadership. He had the bearing of a king. As you develop your leadership skills, don't let your Christian humility keep you bowed down in the corner. Stand up straight, walk with confidence, speak with conviction. (ITS/107)

BEDROOMS

One Christian speaker told me that her bedroom is always a mess because she does all her studying and correspondence in there so it won't show. The living room is lovely, but the bedroom is a clutter. How about your bedroom? Is it a restful, relaxing retreat for you and your husband?

If MGM wanted to make a movie in your town,

would they choose your bedroom for the love scenes? (AEW/146)

BEDTIME

Often complaints of parents about bedtime problems come from those who didn't want to get out of the chair. It's only natural that a child who wasn't tucked in by a parent is going to call for attention. If no one arrives upon demand, the child may well go on a scouting mission. If his appearance in the living room brings forth a parent who will arise like a Phoenix bird from the ashes and chase him to his room, he has achieved his goal.

Even if the parent screams and spanks, the child often prefers that to being ignored. Bad attention is better than none, but wouldn't you prefer to have Junior's last thoughts of you be pleasant and loving rather than hysterical? Remember when you are out of control, the child is in control of your emotions.

Why not get up in the first place, sit with your child on the bed, read him stories, listen to what's on his heart, pray with him, tell him you love him, and give him the security that you will be there in the morning? There's no guarantee he'll never misbehave again, but the odds are with you. (RTC/191-192)

BLAME

If only the other people were perfect, I would be all right! If we were surrounded by delightful people who thought exactly as we did and were excited by our every suggestion, life would be much more pleasant. Unfortunately, this utopia will never come true, and we must grow up to accept the personalities around us as they are.

One morning as I came out to breakfast, Freddie, who was nine at the time, walked in the door from the patio. I said, "Well, Freddie, how are things going with you this morning?" He sighed, "Pretty good so far—I haven't run into any people yet." (AEW/38)

□　　□　　□

Our Freddie first heard my lesson on maturity when he was five years old, and I was amazed at how quickly he got the point when I overheard this dialogue on the patio:

Freddie: "Who broke the wheels off my truck?"

Kevin: "Kenny did it."

John: "Kenny's not even here."

Freddie: "Don't you know that putting the blame on others is a sign of immaturity?" (AEW/39)

□　　□　　□

As Fred and I became aware of our manifold immaturities, we determined to grow up and bring our children along with us. We stopped blaming others for our problems and made the children own up to their mistakes. When we asked them a question, they had only two choices—yes or no. They were not allowed to skirt the issue with "Those kids down the street were over" or "I think the dog did it." They had to own up, accept the blame, and say "I'm sorry. It was my fault."

One night Fred and I came home late and found the following note taped on our mirror from our twelve-year-old Marita:

> *Gee, Dad*
> *I'm really sorry.*
> *Please pray with*
> *me that I will not be tempted*
> *to disobey the rules.*
> *Love, Marita*

While we were grateful for this spiritual confession, what was missing? What was it that she had done? My sanguine nature wanted to wake her up and ask her, but Fred said, "The morning will be soon enough to find out." I could hardly wait until morning, when she told us she had ridden her minibike way up into the hills where the signs said, "No trespassing during fire season." She knew she was wrong and she had accepted the blame before we even knew what she had done.

In recent years I overheard Marita reviewing this principle with Freddie: "The sooner you learn to confess your fault to them *before* they catch you, the better off you'll be." And then she sighed, "I have learned this from bitter experience."

We have all learned together what it means to grow up, and not to put the blame for our failures on others. (AEW/39-40)

□   □   □

Abraham Lincoln said, "I am responsible to the American people, to the Christian world, to history, and on my final account, to God." He was mature. He accepted the overwhelming responsibility that history gave him and was willing to shoulder the blame for his mistakes. Why can't we be mature enough to say, "It was my fault; I'm truly sorry"? That takes a big person, the kind of person that God can be pleased with in eternity. (AEW/47)

BUSYNESS

Sometimes we're in such a hurry that if we came face to face with God in a burning bush, we'd not notice and we'd pass him by.

We want to enjoy our journey, but we don't want to skim over the top so quickly that when we get home we have no memories but a few snapshots of Moses. (LFG/36)

□   □   □

Let's spend time with God today; tomorrow may be too late. There are no instant arks; they take time to build. Let's get to know the Master Builder so he'll keep us afloat. He's no fairweather friend, but he wants to get to know us NOW! (LFG/57)

C

CHILDREN

While Barbie and Ken start life as adults and are obviously self-sufficient, the little babes found in the Cabbage Patch need help. Each one looks so pathetic once you see it in a store that you can't leave it on a shelf to fend for itself. You know it can't face the hard, cruel world alone. (OCP/27)

□   □   □

Never underestimate the power you have to program the computer mind in your child. What you put in will later come out. Do not give up because your child doesn't hang on your every word. They don't even want you to know they've heard what you've said, but *they have.* Keep feeding the machine. (ITS/35)

□   □   □

Without an understanding of the personalities, we fall into the pattern of expecting all parents to be disciplined leaders working lovingly with obedient children. When we personally have neither of these norms, we think we are the only ones in the world who are failures; but as you can see, there are sixteen possible combinations and no two will function identically. Worse than that thought is that if you have four children, they may all be different! What you learned by trial and error with the first one may not work with the others! Once you grasp what personality each member of your family possesses, you will be able to look at each one separately, understand their strengths and weaknesses as well as your own and your mate's, and begin to pull the cast together. (RTC/51)

□   □   □

Part of helping your children to mature is allowing them to make more major choices as they get older. When Fred was sixteen he announced that he wanted to buy a motorcycle with his own money. There's probably not one of you mothers reading this who would get excited over that prospect. Father Fred set a time for our cycle conference, as we made pro-and-con lists. We had all the cons:

WE: You won't want to ride it when it rains.

FRED: I love a motorcycle in the rain.

WE: You'll want to borrow a car for dates.

FRED: I'll only date girls who like to ride on motorcycles. (What a terrible thought! I pictured him tooling up the drive with some Amazon wearing a helmet.)

WE: You'll never get your money back.

FRED: You can always sell a bike for more than you paid for it.

We went over all of our ideas and then let him make the choice. I wish I could say our brilliance swayed him, but it didn't. He chose to buy the cycle. We didn't nag him about it; we just accepted his choice.

When fall came it started to rain. One day he said, "I hate riding this thing in the rain."

As any normal mother, I couldn't resist saying, "Don't you remember? You love motorcycling in the rain."

Saturday night came and he commented, "I can't take this girl out on a motorcycle."

"Why not? You only date girls who like cycles."

"Well, this one doesn't."

Was I glad!

Finally on a rainy Saturday night, Fred said, "Okay, you've won!"

"Won what, Fred?"

"I'm sick of this bike."

"Well, you have nothing to worry about, since you can always sell it for more than you paid for it!"

"I tried to, but nobody wanted it for any price."

Fred made a choice, and he learned to regret it. He has never wanted a motorcycle again.

Please realize that I'm not telling you to let your sons have motorcycles; I'm just teaching the principle that sooner or later we have to let our children make decisions that may not be the best. We show them each side and let them have the choice. (GAD/154-155)

□   □   □

Remember that you can bring up your children in the best house in town and send them to Christian schools, but if they have no feeling of who they are or what they might become, they can still stray from the fold when they reach their teen years. Every hour you spend face-to-face with your children is an investment that only you can make and that, ultimately, will pay dividends. (RTC/77)

CHOLERICS/POWERFULS

The first time the little Powerful babies yelled for a bottle and mother came running, they knew they could take control. It was not a matter of could they, or would they, but when could they take the whole house away from mother. The Baby Powerfuls invented "demand feeding." They soon found that adults were willing to let them have their own way, and if their wishes were not quickly fulfilled, they could get instant action by throwing themselves on the floor and screaming. This threat of a temper tantrum, especially in front of company or in supermarkets, would bring the entire family to its feet in obedience.

Once control had been established, the little Powerfuls only had to use manipulative skills when faced with defiance from family or friends. Because the Powerfuls were all born leaders, they dictated the rules for every game, made definitive choices for every hesitant person, and were put in charge when the teacher had to leave the room. The Powerfuls won the games and earned the letters; they were outstanding members of the debating team and could argue equally well for either side of any issue. (PPO/21)

□   □   □

Powerfuls don't want to spend time thinking about action, as the Perfects do, or talking about action, as the Populars do, or avoiding action, as the Peacefuls do. They want to act now and take a chance that their program will work. (PPO/22)

□   □   □

In the theatrical productions of life the Powerfuls want to direct every drama or play the part of Superman. If they can't run the show, they won't play the game. (PPO/23)

□   □   □

The Cholerics are similar to the Sanguines in that they are both outgoing and optimistic. The Choleric can communicate openly with people, and he knows everything will turn out all right — as long as he's in charge. He gets more done than other temperaments, and he lets you know clearly where he stands. Because the Choleric is goal oriented and has innate leadership qualities, he usually rises to the top in whatever career he chooses. (PPL/58)

□   □   □

The Choleric straightens pictures in other people's houses and polishes the silver in restaurants. One day, when I was at a Sanguine friend's home, helping her with the dishes, I noticed her silver drawer was full of crumbs and the silver all mixed up. Without thinking of what I was doing, I dumped out all the silver, cleaned the divided tray, and sorted the pieces all out into the proper compartments. When she viewed all the forks in one section and the spoons neatly in another, she blinked and said, "Now I see why those trays have all those little sections. I never understood before." (PPL/61)

□   □   □

The Cholerics have a difficult role in life. They have the answers; they know what to do; they can make quick decisions; they bail others out—*but* they are rarely popular because their assurance and assertiveness make others feel insecure, and their ability to lead can easily make them appear bossy. By understanding the temperaments, Cholerics should try to moderate their actions, so that others will rejoice in the Choleric's obvious abilities and not be offended by them. (PPL/62)

□   □   □

Some Cholerics are so anxious to keep tight control that they only delegate the menial tasks—the "dummy work"—and save the grand plan for themselves. Carried to extremes, this protection of control keeps them from achieving as much as they could have done had they learned to deal with people and delegate more wisely. (PPL/65)

□   □   □

While the Sanguine needs friends for an audience,

and the Melancholy needs friends for support, the Choleric doesn't need friends at all. It's not that the Choleric is unfriendly; he just doesn't need anyone around. He has his projects, and he considers socializing a waste of time because it is not accomplishing anything. The Choleric will work for group activity when it has a purpose, and will be glad to jump in and organize your fund drive, but he has no need to spend time in idle chatter. (PPL/66)

□   □   □

As I was in the middle of a message at the Shrine Auditorium in Indianapolis, a thirty-piece bagpipe band struck up "The Campbells Are Coming" right behind stage. I was completely drowned out, and while the chairman fled to quiet the pipes, I created a new twist to my talk. Soon the notes wound down as air coming out of a tire, and the chairman announced the Shriners' Marching Band had been practicing for Saturday's parade without knowing we were only a wall away. Quickly I mentioned how appropriate it was to have a Scottish band as a musical interlude while I spoke, for my mother, Katie MacDougall, once played the bagpipes and marched in her kilts. I then finished my life story with an ethnic twist relating to my Scottish roots.

Oh, how Cholerics love emergencies, so they can rise to unexpected situations and lead off in new directions, especially when accompanied by a thirty-piece bagpipe band. (PPL/67)

□   □   □

The Cholerics are born leaders. They can organize, motivate, delegate, and stimulate. They exude confidence and can run anything. However, they come across as bossy, strong-willed, impetuous, and impatient. They love controversy, manipulate others, and look down on the dummies of life. Their aim is: Do it my way now. Their compulsion is to right all wrongs. They usually marry Phlegmatics because they are easygoing, agreeable, and relaxed, and then get furious when they won't get out of the chair to move. (GAD/38-39)

□   □   □

Cholerics are born with an urge to take charge, and as they grow up they run everything they touch. They usually excel, usually win, and usually are right. This pattern puts them out in front, but doesn't lead to popularity. (GAD/55)

□   □   □

The Choleric's gift for quick, incisive leadership is desperately needed in every phase of life today; *but* carried to extremes, the Choleric becomes bossy, controlling, and manipulative. (PPL/83)

□   □   □

Realize that they look down on weakness and respect strength, so if a Choleric is pushing you around, probably he thinks you're pushable. (GAD/57)

□   □   □

Cholerics want to be perfect and will change quickly if approached positively. Sometimes we bottle up what bothers us and then explode over some triviality. This outburst shows the other person how unstable we are and almost never has a positive effect. (GAD/58)

☐　☐　☐

Don't be the kind of person who looks for a Choleric to take charge and then is critical when he does. (GAD/61)

☐　☐　☐

As the Sanguines see their weaknesses as trivial, and the Melancholies see them as real and hopeless, the Cholerics refuse to believe there is anything about them that could be offensive. Because of their basic premise that they are always right, they naturally can't see that they could possibly be wrong. (PPL/115)

☐　☐　☐

During the break at a marriage seminar one evening, a Choleric man came charging up the aisle, waving his temperament papers in the air.

"I have all of these strengths and none of the weaknesses," he shouted. Behind him was a little Phlegmatic wife, shaking her head *no* but not daring to utter a word.

"Furthermore," he said, "these things aren't even weaknesses."

"What do you mean?" I asked.

"Well, look at this word *impatience.* I would never get impatient if everybody would do what I told them to when I told them to do it!" He pounded the lectern for Choleric emphasis, and in words only a Choleric can say with a straight face, he concluded, "Impatience is not a weakness in me; it is a fault in others." (PPL/115)

□   □   □

The Choleric is a great worker and can accomplish more than any other temperament, but on the negative side, he just can't relax. He goes full steam ahead so long that he can't quite throw the switch and turn himself off. Since Fred and I are both half-Choleric, you can imagine the activity we generate. If we sit down, we feel guilty. Life was made for constant achievements and production.

Every house was made to be changed.

Every meal could be better.

Every drawer could be neater.

Every job could be done faster.

The Choleric in us makes us go, go, go. Don't ever sit down if there's something you can stand up and do! (PPL/116)

□   □   □

Cholerics have to realize that even though we love work, our compulsion for accomplishment puts a terrible pressure on those around us. They are made to feel that if they aren't driving every minute, they're second-class citizens. Cholerics must work at not becoming workaholics so people can enjoy being with them, and not have to run away to keep from having a nervous breakdown. (PPL/119)

❑   ❑   ❑

One of the most dramatic weaknesses of the Choleric is his firm conviction that he is right and those who don't see things his way are wrong. He always knows how to do everything the quickest and the best, and he tells you so. If you don't happen to respond, you are at fault. The Choleric spends much of his time standing on the top of the world, looking down at what he often calls the "dummies of life." This superior attitude can do psychological damage to those under the Choleric's domain. (PPL/120)

❑   ❑   ❑

The Cholerics love controversy and arguments and whether they play it for fun or for serious, this stirring up problems is an extremely negative characteristic. (PPL/126)

❑   ❑   ❑

It is very difficult to counsel the Choleric because he can always prove why what he did was right. Since he is perfect, if it weren't the correct thing to do, he would not have done it. The Choleric just can't be wrong. He cannot admit to his inner self that he just might possibly be at fault. This unbending opinion makes dealing with a

Choleric close to impossible at times. (PPL/126)

□ □ □

Since the Choleric has the greatest potential as a leader for the greatest causes, he should gain the most from the study of the temperaments. He should be able to take his dynamic strengths of quick, decisive action and move to eradicate his sins of conceit and impatience.

But the Choleric is his own worst enemy. He has tattooed the word *strength* on his right arm, and he thinks the word *weakness* belongs only to others. It is this refusal to look at any possible fault in his own make-up that keeps the Choleric from achieving the heights within his grasp.

Shakespeare often wrote of the great hero marred by a tragic flaw. In the Choleric the tragic flaw is his inability to see that he has any. He is more interested in being right than being popular, and when he takes a stand he is inflexible. (PPL/128)

□ □ □

If only the Choleric would open his mind to examine his weaknesses and admit he had a few, he could become the perfect person he thinks he is. (PPL/128)

□ □ □

Once you learn to recognize a Choleric, you will know how to deal with one in a social situation. Ask him difficult questions and be openly impressed with his answers. Nod intelligently at his major truths of life, and he will remember you as a brilliant conversationalist. (PPL/164)

□   □   □

Cholerics are so strong, those dealing with them have to counter with similar strength. They don't mean to force their own way, they just quickly see the logical answer to situations and assume you want what's "right." Once you understand their thinking pattern you can stand firm, and they will respect you for this position. When you allow the Choleric to push you around, he will continue to do so. (PPL/175)

Choleric/Powerful Parent

Because the *Powerful Parent* instantly becomes commander-in-chief in any situation, being in charge of the family seems a natural for them. All they have to do is line up the troops and give orders. It all sounds so simple. Cholerics believe that if everyone would only do things their way now we could all live happily ever after. The Powerful father is accustomed to giving firm orders in the business world without anyone second-guessing him, and he expects the same respect at home. The Powerful mother, usually married to a Peaceful man who wouldn't dream of disagreeing with her, controls the family firmly, and her quick decisions are usually right. The home with a Powerful Parent is usually businesslike and fast-paced unless someone stages an insurrection. (RTC/44)

□   □   □

When two Powerfuls live together there are three alternatives. The most pleasant one is that they both agree and their march toward the goal is done to the same drumbeat. This is possible when, for example, a strong, athletic father produces a son who has similar desires and they mutually dedicate their lives to sports. Even though this provides a positive relationship with this pair, their mutual goals and admiration may be so close that the other children, and sometimes the wife, feel left out and inferior. (RTC/45)

□   □   □

When the controlling parent deals with the sensitive child, his main aim must be to lift up the spirit of this little one and not crush him. Because the Melancholy child is deeply emotional and likes to think things over rather than leap into instant responses, the Powerful Parent is apt to jump on this child and expect quick action. Since the Perfect child is easily intimidated, acts of aggression will immobilize his ability to move at all. Because the strong parent spouts off and then puts the incident behind him, he or she can't believe that three days later the Melancholy child is still brooding over something they've long forgotten. (RTC/49)

□   □   □

The Powerful Parent loves the Peaceful child because by nature he is a follower and is most willing of all to do what the strong parent tells him. Since his inner desire is to avoid any sign of conflict, he wants to do what will make [the parent] happy. Since the Powerful Parent's aim is to keep people under control, he will rejoice in the child's spirit of obedience. This combination is what we tend to think of as the norm. (RTC/51)

□   □   □

The Powerful Parent with the fun-loving Popular child can be an excellent combination. One gets the work done while the other entertains. Since the Popular child is looking for love in both right and wrong places, the Powerful Parent with an understanding of this emotional need can win his child's undying affection if he lets him know clearly what is expected behavior and then praises him lavishly when he performs anywhere close to form. Sanguine, talkative children are motivated by compliments and approval and devastated by criticism. Appreciate their humor, don't make fun of them, and give them plenty of loving and "treat them kind," for a good child nowadays "is hard to find!" (RTC/53)

Choleric-Melancholy

The Choleric-Melancholy temperament is a complementary blend, a combination which fits well together and completes the lacks in each other's natures. The Choleric-Melancholy makes the best business person because the combination of Choleric leadership, drive, and goals with the Melancholy's analytical, detail-conscious, schedule-oriented mind is unbeatable. Nothing is beyond the range of this combination, and they will be successful no matter how long it takes. If they set out to remake a mate, they will keep it up until they have a perfect product. (PPL/143)

□   □   □

Since both temperaments are controlling and creative, the Choleric-Melancholy's inner desire is to remake people and situations to their specifications. (GAD/76)

□   □   □

The Choleric-Melancholy only wants to correct wrongs and bring others up to his high standards. (GAD/77)

□   □   □

Choleric-Melancholy women try to remake their husbands and are very influential in producing children in their image, no matter what the child's own temperament may be. They always like the child best who shows enthusiasm for their constant direction, and they spend less time with the one who shows no desire to be a "before-and-after" example. They mold one and consider the other to be rebellious. (GAD/77).

CHRISTIAN WOMEN

Today's Christian woman is utterly confused. The world is telling her to swing and switch. The books are warning her to look out for number 1. Magazine covers show the typical woman to be stripped to the waist. Newspapers do features on women who left the diapers for instant success on the Board of Directors for General Motors. Television glorifies infidelity as it shows the normal woman having a midday rendezvous in a suite at the Century Plaza—no more tawdry times in a cheap motel.

In contrast to the Playboy Bunny image, feminists say that we should no longer be sex objects. We should wear flat shoes, a hat like Bella Abzug, and march a lot. We should demand our rights, carry big signs, and look on abortions as we do going to the dentist.

Then we go to church and the women are blank-faced with no make-up and so serious as to be depressing. They look as if they were in the running for "Evangelical Frump of the Year Award."

But this will change, for the bulletin announces a new class to be held in the church basement starting next Thursday. Its title, "Sex and Spirituality," promises to make the plain provocative and the sad seductive. One imagines returning six months hence and seeing the congregation full of transformed nymphs wearing lace negligees trimmed with black marabou to match their Bibles.

What's a Christian woman to do? It's all too confusing! As with every other personal problem, we have to get back to the Bible and find out what it really says, for while the world's standards fluctuate, the Bible is the same yesterday, today, and tomorrow. (AEW/97-98)

□   □   □

Wouldn't you like to be a rarity, far above rubies? There is such a *need* for leadership today, so many cries for direction. We need women who are willing to say, "Here am I, use me." We need older women to teach the young. We *need*

women who are examples for others to follow

women who are willing to take a chance

women who will encourage others

women who aren't touchy or petty

women who can think beyond the moment

women who have the attitude and bearing of a leader

women who try to look their best

women who can call a meeting to order

women who will open their homes

women who have compassion for those in trouble

women who are ready to pursue excellence.

There are so few virtuous women around, so few pursuing excellence in either the world or the average church. Are you willing to read these pages, spend some time on introspection and reflective thinking, set some new goals?

Let's stand out as a rarity and reach for a crown of rubies. (ITS/11)

CHURCH

The church has to forget its middle-of-the-road, look-the-other-way attitude and start teaching God's laws on sex and marriage. The evangelical churches have pretended there is no problem. One pastor told me, "We try to look the other way because we don't want to embarrass anyone." (GAD/80)

CLOTHING

The Bible tells us our beauty should not depend upon our outward adornment. And yet the virtuous woman of Proverbs 31 was clothed in tapestries of scarlet and in purple silks. She had that look of quiet elegance befitting a queen. How about us? (ITS/109)

□   □   □

Try on your clothes and ask yourself, "What do I see?" If you have an outfit that compliments your natural color, if no part of it stands out and your shoes blend with the total look, you are probably all right. (ITS/110)

□   □   □

When God appointed Aaron to be the high priest, the spiritual leader, He said, "Make special clothes for Aaron to indicate his separation; beautiful garments that will lend dignity to his work" (Exodus 28:2, TLB). Begin to build a wardrobe of special clothes that will add dignity to your work. (ITS/110)

COMFORT

How pathetic that Christians who should give comfort so often feel it's God's appointment to heap guilt on the one in need. When you are the victim of one of life's calamities, you don't need pious platitudes placing blame. Comfort, don't convict. (ITS/162)

□   □   □

Psalm 9:20 is a plaintive verse: "I looked for someone to take pity, but there was none; and for comforters but I found none." This verse describes some of those in our Christian community. People with buckets of burdens looking for people with armloads of answers but finding few real comforters, few who are ready to give cheer in time of grief. This lack of desire to help is especially noticed in the areas of "unpopular problems" such as rape, incest, and child molestation. (ITS/165)

□   □   □

God wants us to have our eyes open, to comfort his people, to relieve the afflicted. ABOVE AVERAGE women are all in demand. Isaiah 50:4 says, "The Lord hath given me the tongue of the learned, that I should know how to speak a word in season to him that is weary." What can we do to comfort the depressed, the defenseless, the diseased, the dying? (ITS/166)

□   □   □

Remember, the God of peace comforts us not so we'll become comfortable, but so we will comfort others. (LFG/130)

□   □   □

What a comfort to know that God is real and that He is our *defense,* our *dwelling place,* and our source of *direction* when we lift up our eyes to Him. (LFG/143)

□   □   □

Sometimes our greatest ministry to one in bereavement or one waiting through a loved one's surgery is to just be there and be sensitive. (ITS/168)

□   □   □

Average people often say, "If there's anything I can do, let me know." ABOVE AVERAGE people do something specific. (ITS/168)

COMMUNICATION

One night Fred said, "We haven't had enough time to converse with each other. Let's set aside the hour after dinner and go to our room alone."

"You mean before you do your phoning?" I asked.

The first night I talked nonstop for over an hour, the second night an hour, the third night thirty minutes, and by the fourth night I didn't have much to say. It was amazing how my feelings changed. Once I knew Fred would listen, I no longer had a compulsion to converse. (AEW/138)

□   □   □

When we are dating we all feel free to converse because we know the other person will receive our words open-mindedly. They want to get to know us and they listen with attention. But as we begin to function in the closeness of marriage, we begin to find negative reactions to some of our favorite subjects. The more fearful we become of pushing our partner in an adverse direction, the less we communicate. Because we are afraid of a bad reaction, we tend to share our true feelings only with outsiders who will listen. (AEW/170)

□   □   □

If you men want to open up communication, try to agree with [women] in some area quickly. This will unnerve us and give you an immediate advantage. Because most of you love to argue with us and put us down, we are stunned by a man who agrees with us on anything. Arguing builds up barriers between us. Agreement tears them down. You don't need a wall when you're both on the same side.

This simple principle of agreement, when applied, will be a blessing in your marriage. In Amos 3:3 it says, "Can two walk together except they be agreed?"

In the past Fred found something wrong with everything I said. He was so predictable that I would carry on mock conversations in my mind with him. As soon as I would hear him disagree, I would file that thought away in the reject pile, never to be dealt with again. What a big pile of resentment I built up, a barrier to communication! (AEW/180)

□   □   □

The majority of the couples I counsel don't hate each other but are just emotionally divorced. They stopped communicating somewhere along the line and neither side did anything about it. Don't let this happen to you. Don't wait for your wife to come in hysterical; plan relaxing times when you can get away together and communicate. Don't take friends or relatives along. Don't go on a tour with twenty-four-hour activities. Go to a quiet motel and renew acquaintances.

Some couples who do not force themselves to sit down and discuss their poor communication never know until it's too late where they missed out. (AEW/181)

□   □   □

Some of you may have spent so many years building your walls of interruption, depression, anger, false agreement, joking, ridicule, defensiveness, or silence to fence off your own area of Private Property that it would take King Arthur and his entire court to knock down your fortress. You have learned how to fend off invaders with your weapons and you've successfully kept your mate at a distance. You communicate on your terms on your topics at your time. You've established a pattern and you don't know how to change. (AEW/190)

□   □   □

In our small group sessions in CLASS [Christian Leaders and Speakers Seminars], each participant is asked to introduce himself or herself. We don't ask them to bare their souls, and yet within a matter of minutes people are sharing their needs openly in front of a group of people they don't even know. Why? Because so many have been stuffing their concerns down inside them, assuming that no one else has any problems or that the Christian community would judge them as less than spiritual if they opened their mouths. Given an opportunity to honestly state how they feel, the words pour out like a waterfall. (OCP/47)

COMPLIMENTS

Even though Paul thought of it first, Carnegie's basic principle for winning friends is to give compliments, to find something genuinely good in everyone. (GAD/133-134)

□   □   □

To compliment we first have to "notice." We have to open our preoccupied minds and take the blinders off our glazed eyes. As I travel I look for people who could use encouragement. One day I noticed a lady in line at the ticket counter at Los Angeles Airport who had on an ordinary housedress and was carrying a shopping bag. As I glanced her way I saw she had silver-etched, heart-shaped buttons down the front of the dress. "What beautiful buttons you have!" I commented. She looked up and beamed.

"My friend brought these home from Germany and I made the whole dress to go with the buttons. You're the first one who's noticed them."

Start today on a compliment course. Practice on everyone you meet. You can always praise the buttons. Be the first one to notice what's good. "If there be any virtue, and if there be any praise, think [and comment] on these things" (Philippians 4:8).

Think now of some person who troubles you

much. The next time you see that body heading your way, look for the buttons. Quickly find something genuinely positive to compliment. It's hard for that person to tackle you when you've started on a gracious note. (GAD/136)

□   □   □

Not one of us wants to be criticized, yet we seem equally uncomfortable with praise. Some of us have been knocked down so long that we don't feel we deserve a compliment and some of us doubt that any positive person is really telling the truth. Where does this negative attitude place the positive person? How does this kind and uplifting individual feel when he has given a compliment and the recipient's response ranges from uneasy silence to vehement denial?

How about a hypothetical compliment: "That's a lovely linen suit you're wearing today." Some possible responses:

— "This old thing?"

— "This isn't linen; it's just rayon."

— "I picked it up at Goodwill."

— "It's a reject from my sister."

Any of these comments show I have no taste and remind me never to say a nice word to you again.

Many ladies complain that their husbands never give them compliments. One man summed it up when he said, "I used to tell her how good she looked and she'd always make me feel like a dummy for saying so. Finally I quit noticing anything and now she complains."

A dentist complimented his receptionist, "Your

hair looks great today."

She retorted, "What was wrong with it yesterday?"

We mean to be humble but we insult the intelligence of the givers when we refuse their compliments. How much happier we can make others when we express gratitude for their comments. (ITS/37-38)

□　　□　　□

If you have been led to believe by your parents or your church that to accept any affirmation is unspiritual, that self-deprecation is next to godliness, that any feeling of frivolity is sinful, that you are to pick up your cross daily and drag it through life, perhaps this is the time for you to step on the worm of unworthiness. Religious people often portray a grim picture of piety, but a look in God's Word shows the value of encouragement and the virtue of a joyful heart. Don't let a legalistic background hamper your happiness and your ability to accept a compliment. When you throw down a silver box that has been offered, the donor doesn't see this rejection as spiritual, but as a personal affront. (BOX)

□　　□　　□

From the time I was a child I remember seeking my mother's approval. I always did well in everything I tackled, and I knew enough not to attempt sports, art, or music because I had no talent in these areas. My mind could learn the rules, principles, or keyboard, but my body wouldn't cooperate. My mother, a violin and cello teacher, was disappointed that I couldn't even hold the

69

bow correctly, so I set out to excel where I could. I got good grades and hoped that Mother would praise me.

Once when I asked her why she didn't tell other people how well I was doing in school after Peggy's mother had bragged about her, she replied, "You never know when you'll have to eat your words."

Throughout life I've tried to pull a compliment out of Mother, but, while she was never negative, she hung in at neutral. One day within the past year I came home after a frustrating visit. I'd shown Mother my exciting schedule of speaking, including a European trip, a Cancun retreat, and an Alaskan cruise. Her response was, "It's amazing you're so busy considering what you do is something nobody needs."

I was discouraged and I told Fred of this comment. He looked up and said, "When are you going to grow up and be able to function without your Mother's approval?" I was shocked at this question. I *was* grown-up, and my success didn't depend on my mother's approval—or did it?

Fred continued, "How old is your mother?"

"Eighty-five."

"Has she praised you much before?"

"No."

"Then what makes you think she'll start today? If she hasn't been excited about your life before, what makes you expect she'll change now? Why don't you stop trying to impress her, and just love her as she is? Isn't that what you teach others?"

I wish I could say I enjoyed Fred's analysis and that I was so spiritual that I leaped for his solution. Instead, I just kept quiet and thought about it. But the more I thought about it, the more I realized he was right. My mother is a Phlegmatic personality not given to enthusiasm or vain praises. I am part Sanguine, wanting credit and applause for what I do. How childish of me, understanding the different temperaments well, to be seeking for something my mother's nature couldn't give.

As the truth sank into me I realized a principle in getting along with people: *We should give them what they desire and not be looking for them to fill our needs.* (GAD/161-162)

COMPROMISE

Compromise means "promise together, make a mutual pledge, come in from the extremes and meet on a common ground." Compromise is a proven tool in getting along with difficult people, and yet as individuals we resist using it because underneath we'd really like to have our own way. (GAD/148)

◻   ◻   ◻

A Choleric woman told me about the battle she was having with her Choleric ten-year-old son. Every day after he goes to school, she goes in and moves the furniture in his room into the position where she and the decorator want it. The first thing he does when he comes home is change it all back to the way he likes it. She maintains it's her house and she has the right to put the furniture wherever she wants it. Besides, what if her friends came to visit, and the room wasn't in order! He, being a chip off the old block, claims his room as his ter-

71

ritory where he has the right to arrange it whatever way he wants. Here are two Cholerics fighting so hard for control that they are playing Mayflower Movers every day. I shared with her how important it is for a Choleric child to be in control of something at home, for if he is thwarted there, he will likely go out and beat up his friends. With this new thought in mind, she went home to make peace. (YPT/44)

◻   ◻   ◻

When Marita was thirteen it was the era of tie-dyed T-shirts and frayed jeans. Even though I had grown up in the Depression and had no money for clothes I had never dressed this poorly. One day I saw her out in the driveway rubbing the hems of her new jeans with dirt and rocks. I was aghast at her ruining these pants I had just paid for and ran out to tell her so. She continued to grind on as I recounted my soap opera of childhood deprivation in the driveway. As I concluded without having moved her to tears of repentance, I asked why she was wrecking her new jeans. She replied without looking up, "You can't wear new ones."

"Why not?"

"You just can't, so I'm messing them up to make them look old." Such total loss of logic! How could it be the style to ruin new clothes?

Each morning as she would leave for school I would stare at her and sigh, "My daughter looking like that." There she'd stand in her father's old T-shirt, tie-dyed with big blue spots and streaks. Fit for a duster, I thought. And those jeans—so low-slung I feared if she took a deep breath they'd drop off her rear. But where would they go? They were so tight and stiff they couldn't move. The frayed bottoms, helped by the rocks, had strings that dragged behind her as she walked.

One day after she had left for school, it was as if the Lord got my attention and said, "Do you realize what your last words are to Marita each morning? 'My daughter looking like that.' When she gets to school and her friends talk about their old-fashioned mothers who complain all the time, she'll have your constant comments to contribute. Have you ever looked at the other girls in junior high? Why not give them a glance?"

I drove over to pick her up that day and observed that many of the other girls looked worse. On the way home I mentioned how I had overreacted to her ruining her jeans. I offered a compromise: "From now on you can wear anything you want to school and with your friends, and I won't bug you about it."

"That'll be a relief."

"But when I take you out with me to church or shopping or to my friends, I'd like you to dress in something you know I like without my having to say a word."

She thought about it.

Then I added, "That means you get 95 percent your way and I get 5 percent for me. What do you think?"

She got a twinkle in her eye as she put out her hand and shook mine. "Mother, you've got yourself a deal!"

From then on I gave her a happy farewell in the morning and didn't bug her about her clothes. When I took her out with me, she dressed properly without fussing. We had ourselves a deal! (GAD/149-150)

□   □   □

Sometimes we create our own special difficult people by insisting that they do it our way *now*.

A spirit of compromise softens hard people. (GAD/152)

CONCERN

If we really want to get along with other people, we don't need to worry about our externals—we have to rededicate our *internals* to showing genuine concern for others. (GAD/141)

□   □   □

Difficult people are always hurting inside, but they cover it up by being rude, defensive, or withdrawn. Don't accept them at face value, but instead be the one who takes the time to show genuine concern. (GAD/144)

CONFESSION

God tells us clearly, "If we confess our sins, he is faithful and just to forgive us our sins and to cleanse us from all unrighteousness." He then adds (in case we don't think we've really been unrighteous), "If we say that we have not sinned, we make him a liar, and his word is not in us" (1 John 1:9,10).

Even though you are obviously a very good person, what is there about you that is offensive to others?

Where do you need improvement? What habit have you been unable to break? What has just come to your mind? Confess this to the Lord and He will free you from this bondage. Don't hide it any longer—bring it out into the open before the Lord and He will give you forgiving peace. (AEW/88-89)

□   □   □

It is possible to grow as a Christian and yet not deal with uncleansed areas of our life, but we never have a clear conscience until we have pulled out the hidden sins and placed them before the Lord with a confessing heart. Perhaps you've left some sin in your life festering in a corner. Perhaps you've rationalized why it's not your fault at all. Perhaps you've shoved it into a closet but the stench keeps seeping out.

Don't try to keep your failures under wraps. Bring them out in the open and confess them to the Lord. He never gossips or tells tales. You can trust the truth with Him! (AEW/90)

□   □   □

Perhaps you've been trying to get close to God, but you haven't *left Egypt.* Perhaps you have some destructive habits that you are unwilling to give up. Perhaps you have some "secret sins" that no one knows about so you haven't been disciplined to change. Perhaps you're too busy with the pleasures of Egypt to spend any time with the Lord . . . Is God calling you out of Egypt into the desert where he can get your attention? . . . Give him a try; make a decision, for *leaving Egypt* is the

75

first step in finding God. (LFG/137-139)

CONFIDENCE

There's no better way to seal an agreement than to let the person know you have confidence in his attitude and his wisdom. (GAD/127)

□   □   □

When you have a human-relations problem, don't run away or weep and wail. Tackle the situation quickly, get to the source of the problem, praise the person for whatever you can find, and let him know you have confidence in him. (GAD/139)

□   □   □

Confidence means a state of trust, reliance, and assurance. I believe in you; I can rely on you; I *know* I can count on you. (GAD/158)

□   □   □

We live in a discouraging world full of people who put us down. What bright lights we can be when we say the simple words, "I have confidence in you!" (GAD/160)

COUNSELING

Much of what passes for Christian counseling

today is putting a large Band-Aid of wishful thinking over a festering wound and then wondering why it doesn't heal. (BBC/204)

□   □   □

Don't be guilty of counseling from ignorance. If you are going to be talking with depressed people, study everything you can find on the subject. (BBC/143)

□   □   □

If you are doing any type of counseling, don't flaunt your wisdom. This is not a glory job; it is a humble opportunity to help a distressed person. Your responsibility is not to be brilliant, but to guide a person in need into making a proper decision. (BBC/151)

□   □   □

Once you have examined the background, you as a counselor will have an understanding of why this particular person has been depressed by this problem. Obviously the people with too much to do or too little to do will respond to different solutions. Knowing where the person has come from will keep you from heading in the wrong direction. (BBC/159)

□   □   □

Never let the person leave you the first time without a glimmer of hope. He must see that there are some possibilities. (BBC/159-160)

□   □   □

When you have established a base of spiritual communication with a person, you can begin to work toward a hopeful future. While it is important to put out today's fires, it is also imperative to prevent them from flaring up again in the future. (BBC/164)

□   □   □

A person must get out of the dream world, accept the situation as it is (not as he wishes it were), and move on from there. If you can get this far with a person, you can then bring his behavior patterns under the guidance of Scripture. (BBC/166)

COVER-UP

What happens after we *doubt* God's Word, are easily *tempted,* enter into *sin,* and feel *guilty?* We're so afraid we'll get caught that we hide from authority and try to cover up the evidence. That's what Adam and Eve did too.

When Freddie was little and knew he had done something wrong, he would run to his bed and put his head under the pillow, assuming that if he hid this way I wouldn't find him. In recent years many politicians have doubted that the law was for them, have been tempted by the allure of power and money, have sinned and felt guilty, and have been caught in their own nets of cover-up. (AEW/57-58)

COVETING

We are told not to desire, long for, or crave something (anything) that belongs to someone else. When I first read this commandment with meaning, I realized I coveted everything I saw. I wanted it all. Coming from a childhood without curtains or even a scatter rug, I longed for drapes and carpeting. I could rationalize that I deserved them, especially if *you* had them. Even though I know better today and I realize that greed is a form of idol worship, if I come to visit you and you have new monogrammed towels, I'll want them. (LFG/155)

□　　□　　□

Coveting is such a subtle sin that most of us don't confess it or even dignify it with a plea for forgiveness; yet, wishing we had more than we have (sometimes misnamed goal-setting, especially when the desire is to possess what our neighbor has) is a sin of great significance to God. (LFG/155)

CRITICISM

What does the person who gives you unsolicited advice expect from you? He expects you will become defensive, lose your Christian cool, and therefore validate his opinion that you have a problem and aren't practicing what you preach. Since you don't want to give him this affirmation of his evaluation, accept his advice cheerfully and thank him for it. This stops him in his tracks in a most positive way and prevents him from proceeding to Points B, C, and D. (ITS/39-40)

79

□   □   □

As you become good at accepting criticism and develop your own style of response, you can then move on to the next step: *Ask for it.* That step is the graduate work in our Christian living. We feel we've made progress when we can first take it, then take it cheerfully. But when the Lord is really in control of our lives. He will prompt us to ask for it. So often in Proverbs it says that a wise man asks for counsel while a fool despises instruction and that if you rebuke a wise man he will love you, but a fool will hate you. If a wise man loves rebuke and I want to be wise, I must look for helpful suggestions. I must ask for evaluation. (ITS/40)

□   □   □

Let's learn to accept suggestions and even insults cheerfully. Let's ask for evaluations and listen thankfully. Let's run them through our mental "fact filter." If they're valid, let's act upon them. If they're of no consequence, let's forget them. (ITS/41)

□   □   □

The more critical a person is, the more desperate is his craving for appreciation. (GAD/147)

□   □   □

When any of us take the time to think about our interchanges with other people, we realize how little honest opinion we encourage. We build our boxes around us, people learn how near they dare come to our fence, and they develop a working relationship with us that may be utterly phony. Does your family have to humor you to keep peace? Do your co-workers know how close they can come before you get mad or moody? If people are having to handle you with kid gloves, maybe it's time you got honest with them and allowed them to be honest with you. (PPL/52)

D

DEPRESSION

Many women I talk with start each day with a little black cloud hovering over their pillow. Some choose to turn over, pull up the blankets, and escape through sleep. Others get up slowly and plod through a dreary day, believing that the cloud is a normal part of their everyday lives, shadowing their every move. Some jump up quickly and run all day to meetings, appointments, schools, banks, and luncheons, hoping to outrun their little black cloud. But refusing to face the problem or accepting gloom as a way of life or running away from the situation is fruitless: We cannot escape; the little black cloud always returns. (BBC/12)

Symptoms of Depression

Passiveness. This passive nature may be looked upon as an improvement: "Father hasn't yelled at us all week." It's easy to see this first sign of depression as a welcome relief instead of a symptom.

Loss of interest. As the afflicted person becomes less active, his interest in life begins to diminish. As the depressed person tries to become dead to his pain, he becomes dead to joy.

Pessimism. While some people are gloomy by nature, pessimism in a normally positive person is a danger signal.

Hopelessness. With this period comes a plunging down of self-esteem, a feeling that "there is no way out," and depression is sure to follow.

Self-deprecation. When one begins to get this attitude and sees himself as a failure, he becomes depressed.

Withdrawal. At this point the depressed person emotionally withdraws from communicating with other people, followed later by a physical withdrawal.

Preoccupation with self. The depressive person begins to get wrapped up in himself, winding protective layers around his soul to keep from getting hurt.

Dislike of happy people. There is nothing worse for the depressed person than some effervescent optimist shouting, "Let's all cheer up!" This gaiety only sends the distressed person into the pit.

Change of personality and habits. It's a sure sign of depression when someone who was always outgoing and joyful suddenly just does not care.

Fatigue. Overwhelming fatigue causes the depressed person to be too tired to do anything.

Overeating or undereating. These two symptoms seem like contradictions, and although they are opposites, underneath they represent the same problem.

Increase in drinking or drugs. This increase becomes a symptom when someone begins to drink more than he has in the past or starts taking a large number of tranquilizers or sleeping pills to calm him down, or pep pills to get himself going.

Poor concentration. It's extremely difficult for a disturbed person to think clearly, and it is therefore unwise for him or her to make big decisions.

Hypochondria. Many extreme depressants ultimately just take to their beds.

Suicidal tendencies. By the time the depressant has come this far, he begins to seriously debate whether there is any use in living at all.

Sudden improvement. A sudden improvement after a long depression may be a sign that the planned end is near.

The call to death. The last step before suicide is when the depressant wills himself out of reality. He has programmed himself to be in a position where he is beyond it all—in another world, and where he is ready to go to a further world. (BBC/21-31)

Who Gets Depressed?

The born loser starts life knowing he is hopeless. If we bring up our children to believe that they're no good, insignificant, and inferior, and that they don't measure up to others, we'll program our children to be losers.

Successful people can have a tendency toward depression, especially the person who has reached the top and has no more exciting plans ahead.

Those who cannot communicate. If we don't guide our children into a positive pattern of conversation, they will grow up unable to communicate, unable to share their feelings, and carrying deep, bottled-up resentments.

Those who can't compete. Many parents over-protect their children to the point where the child doesn't understand that life is real. When we make things too easy for our children, either on purpose ("So he won't have to go through what I went through") or by benign neglect ("It was easier to just do it for her than teach her"), we do them a great disservice in the guise of charity, and we unknowingly encourage a dependency personality which may turn them to drugs or alcohol.

Those with too much to do. Some women know their priorities are out of order but seem trapped by peer pressure. Exhaustion leads to depression.

Those with nothing to do. Having seen that those with too much to do get discouraged, you might think it a contradiction that those with nothing to do are also depressed and easily bored. Boredom is the baby of depression.

Those in drastic circumstances. In dealing with people in critical circumstances, I have learned that the first step must be an acceptance of the fact. Only when we realistically face the truth can we begin to overcome the hurt and despair. The worst approach is to pretend it never happened. Drastic circumstances can put us into constant depression.

People with serious illness. In the year 1985 much attention was given to "mercy killing" or helping the elderly with fatal diseases to commit suicide. When life as it is seems hopeless, suicide seems to be a positive alternative.

Those with a low self-image. While a correct self-image is desirable, many people grow up with a low self-image. They feel they can't do anything right, they don't look good, or they never know what to say. This poor view of themselves is often instilled by parents who repeatedly tell them they're clumsy, fat, dull, or stupid. What a responsibility we have to make sure our children and our mates do not struggle through defeated, dreary lives! A low self-image leads to depression.

Those with too high standards. Some of us, pushed by either parents or mates, or else driven by our own standards of perfection, set impossible goals for ourselves and become depressed when we cannot make them.

Those who feel guilty. Those who carry deep guilt feelings, for whatever reason, easily become depressed, Hovering guilt clouds settle into depression. (BBC/34-51)

Teen Depression

If a young person feels that even one parent, but preferably both, really accepts him as he is, approves of him as a real person, and gives him eye-to-eye attention at least occasionally, he will not want to end it all.

If he feels support from the family for his various activities and adventures and knows that home is a place of refuge where loving people await him, he will probably return. (BBC/180-181)

Symptoms of Teen Depression

Behavior changes. Any change in attitude—sudden burst of temper, lashing out at family members, withdrawal from usual activities—should be examined as possible depression.

Lowering of grades. Any sudden drop in grades or interest in school may signify depression and/or a use of drugs.

Different friends. When old friends are dropped and new ones either appear to be of a questionable nature or don't appear at all, you should be suspicious of drugs and depression.

Dazed look and bored attitude. These are again symptoms of both depression and some kind of drug use. Since 50 percent of teen suicides are known to be drug-related, these two problems often go hand-in-hand.

Noticeable changes in eating habits. Any eating disorder is a sign of depression: anorexia (starving to get thin enough to satisfy a shaky self-image) or bulimia (gorging on food and then self-inducing vomiting). One girl told me she had been doing this after every meal for two years and her parents had never appeared to notice.

Changes in sleep patterns. Use of drugs can cause constant sleepiness or a hyperactive personality. Even without drugs a severely depressed child will often have trouble sleeping or will seem to be passing out at any possible opportunity. As with adults, the sleep pattern may swing in either direction, but a change means trouble.

Talk of suicide. Before a youngster takes his own life he usually runs the idea by the family to pick up their reaction. If the father says, "Only an idiot would kill himself" and the mother asks, "Why would a good boy like you from a fine family like ours even mention such a thing?" the teen will know that he and his parents are on different planets. If your child brings the subject up, listen and feel out his opinion; ask why teens are doing this. Don't moralize or preach. Remember, he's asking you if you really love him.

Written signals. Frequently the troubled teen will write notes that give clues to his feelings. His school papers may allude to death and he may write practice suicide notes and wait for your reaction. Remember, he doesn't think you care.

Giving away possessions. If a teen starts doling out his radio or his favorite sweater, or making lists of what he wants his friends to have when he's gone, be sure to take this unusual pattern seriously.

Attempted suicide. Once a teen has tried and failed, there is a high probability that he or she will try again. Many parents look at this attempt as an attention-getter, but it should be considered as valid. Check the house for weapons and drugs. When a teen returns from the hospital after an attempted suicide, be aware that this is the time he is most apt to try it again. (BBC/185-186)

Help for Depression

Recognize the problem. To face the reality of our situation, we don't have to put on a T-shirt that says "I'm depressed" or carry a big sign saying, "Stop the world—I want to get off." But we have to admit that we have a problem and know that we must do something about it.

Decide that you need help. In my own counseling I've discovered that many people don't want help even though they've asked for it. Some of those with a low self-image merely want a counselor to agree that their situation is hopeless and put the stamp of approval on a life of martyred misery.

Until a person wants help, there's no point in outlining a solution.

Examine the causes. In order to lift our black

cloud, we must positively and honestly examine the reasons for our depression.

At one point in my life I was overwhelmed with housework. Then I examined the problem and decided I hadn't properly utilized my family's manpower. Inwardly I wanted to do the work myself. This way I could complain that I was overworked and underappreciated!

Look at the alternatives. When we face depression openly, it will usually improve. After you bring it to the surface, seek help from a friend or counselor. At this point it is helpful to look realistically at the alternatives. What possible answers are available?

Check your health. Sometimes depression is caused by some body misfunction. Several years ago I sank into a period of unexplainable exhaustion and could hardly move. When I had to speak I would "psych myself up" and force myself to go, but when it was over I would collapse for hours. Several doctors gave me alternatives: It was either all in my head, a bored housewife syndrome, or a bid for attention. I knew these diagnoses weren't true and persisted until I found a doctor who gave me a five-hour glucose tolerance test. The results showed I had severe hypoglycemia.

Analyze self-pity. When we can prove that "anyone would be depressed in my circumstances," there is little impetus to improve.

Avoid trouble. When we think preventively, we can save ourselves unnecessary grief. Some depressed women are like vacuum cleaners: They suction up bad news all day and then empty it all out on the family at dinner.

Take action. Since depression is a conviction of

one's own helplessness, one human step to relieve this problem is to find some area where you are proficient. Make a goal using your talent and/or desires, then write down steps to achieve this goal. Don't be discouraged when the path looks too difficult. Accept this as part of the challenge. Remember: No goal = no achievement = depression.

Do not fear failure. If you don't enter any races, you can never be a winner.

Get organized. I make use of every set of hands. When Fred was in fifth grade a little boy came to spend a night with him. He enjoyed himself and stayed for a week. On the third day I put his name on the work chart and assigned him jobs. I overheard him tell Fred, "Your mother must really like me. She put my name on the family work chart." When children are shown what to do and are praised for their accomplishments, they become eager helpers.

Aside from making use of available glovepower, what else can you do to get organized? Perhaps you are depressed because you've never finished the housework. Nothing has ever been perfect. I've been married thirty-six years and have never risen clearly above the waters, but with organization, the swimming is easier.

Get your priorities in order. While some women spend too much time alone at home, some stay away if at all possible. Their reasons? Boring housework, demanding husbands, and intolerable children. The depressing results of this flight are that the house gets worse, the husband complains more strongly, and the children have tantrums just to get Mother's attention.

No matter how positive or saintly our activities may be, we must make sure we have our priorities in order. Let's not "lose" our families while "saving" others!

Improve yourself. Some of us after looking in the mirror and seeing the lines of time etched around our eyes do try to hide from our black clouds by pulling the covers over our heads.

Whatever your particular need, start looking for an answer. Write down a list of your goals and find people who can help you. Don't be afraid to ask questions. No one will think you are stupid. Many of us are full of answers waiting for some questions to come our way!

Although physical improvement is not the only solution for depression, it is a good place to start.

Help someone else. Much of our drift into depression comes from preoccupation with self. We are so deeply involved with our own problems that we can't see other people in need; yet when we do help someone else, we get a lift.

No purpose = No accomplishment = Depression.

Review your financial position. There are many depressed women who live in lavish homes, charge their clothes at expensive stores, and drive to the country club in a Cadillac. They have made the great American climb, yet are nervous. They may worry over their husband's business, the second mortgage, or a bank loan. It's surprising how easy it is to be depressed while elegantly gowned at the charity ball if your phone may be disconnected tomorrow. (BBC/53-88)

□   □   □

What do you do when all else fails? If you have done all you know to do and have sought the Lord's will in your life and have still come up empty, perhaps there are some hidden problems in your past that you have not wanted to look at or some events in your childhood that were so traumatic that you blanked them out totally from your conscious memory.

You can't just hide these problems and hope they'll go away; you have to deal with them, work through them, and resolve your feelings. (BBC/203)

□   □   □

We must believe in God, the Father who created us; in Jesus Christ, the Son of God who died for our sins; and in the Holy Spirit, the available power who can change our patterns of life. When we do believe, we can with assurance follow God's plan for overcoming depression. (BBC/97)

□   □   □

Those of us who are happy assume that depressed people want to be happy like us. We try to jolly them up and say, "Life isn't that bad. Look at the bright side of things." But they can't cheer up so easily, and that inability gets them more depressed. They review in their minds all those people who have rejected them in the past and assume that you will do the same. They know they aren't normal, that nobody cares, and that they'd be better off dead. So what do they want?

Improved circumstances.

A friend who won't reject them.

The assurance that they aren't crazy.

A reason for living. (GAD/70-71)

□   □   □

Part of the pattern of depression is the belief that no one really cares, and so when someone appears to, they're looked upon with suspicion. (GAD/71)

□   □   □

Depressed people need a real friend who will be understanding and compassionate, who won't scold, laugh loudly, or put them down. (GAD/72)

□   □   □

Since the depressed person often thinks he's crazy and there's no reason to keep living, you will serve God's purpose if you can be the one to give hope. Show that we as Christian believers don't sorrow as those who have no hope, but that God uses our depressions and trials for ultimate good. (GAD/72)

□   □   □

A person who is seriously depressed functions emotionally at about a third-grade level. Knowing this will keep you from expecting too much. (GAD/73)

□   □   □

Frequently, depressed people want their cir-

93

cumstances improved but are too disturbed to see clear
alternatives. Don't assume that they have analyzed all
possibilities. (GAD/73)

□   □   □

When we understand the basic personalities and
their desires, we can see what causes depression in each
type of person. Take away what we want in life, make us
feel helpless to achieve our goals, and we will become discouraged.

The Sanguines/Populars get depressed when life is
no longer fun and no one is giving them complimentary
attention.

The Melancholies/Perfects get depressed when
things aren't lining up properly and people aren't sensitive to their inner feelings.

The Phlegmatics/Peacefuls get depressed when
they have to face conflict personally (they can always
mediate other people's problems with a cool detachment)
and no one is appreciating their worth.

The Cholerics/Powerfuls become depressed when
any part of their life is out of control, whether it is work,
family, finances, health, or body. (PPO/161)

□   □   □

When for the first time in my life I acknowledged
that my depression was not a natural trait but a sin, God
took the burdens away. He didn't change my circumstances; He just made me able to accept them and get on with
some new direction. Only then did I experience the

release of hopelessness and the enrichment of happiness. (BBC/117)

DIRECTION

It may not take a lot to be above average, but it does take something. It takes desire. Do you care enough to try? It takes a goal. Do you wish to aim high? You've perhaps heard of the airline pilot who announced over the loudspeaker, "I have bad news and good news. The bad news is we're lost and don't know where we're going. The good news is we're making very good time." This simple story represents many of our lives. We're lost, we don't know where we're going, but we're rushing on to get there. (ITS/15)

❑   ❑   ❑

A ninety-six-year-old lady was a faithful attendant at my women's club Bible studies. She came with her lessons prepared and knew all the answers. One day a tactless member asked her, "Why do you work so hard on these lessons when you're so old and it doesn't matter?"

Little Bess Elkins looked up and said confidently, "I'm cramming for my finals."

It's never too late to get ready for our finals. Narrow is the way which leads to life and few there be that find it. It takes so little to be ABOVE AVERAGE, but it does take a desire to learn and it does take preparation so when the great target appears we'll be able to hit the bull's-eye. (ITS/17)

□   □   □

What can you do to help your children become productive adults?

1. Don't depend on the school guidance counselor to steer your child in the right direction. Aptitude testing can give indications of your child's ability, but these standard questions cannot take your place. You know your child's talents and gifts. By now you should have a handle on his personality and know his strengths and weaknesses. Don't let someone else choose his future.

2. Spend time discussing each child's personality. I constantly meet adults who are in the wrong profession because a parent or counselor pushed them without regard to their personality potential. One Sanguine accountant told me he quit his job after hearing me speak because it was the first time he could understand why he hated what he was doing. He went into the travel business and loves being with people day and night. The Popular Sanguine will never be happy with routine work away from people. These people live for excitement, spontaneity, and response from an audience.

The Powerful Choleric will chafe under circumstances where he has no control or even the possibility of promotion somewhere down the line. He will be happiest in his own business or at least in a position where he can see steps of advancement.

The Perfect Melancholy doesn't do well in a place where dealing with people is the main objective, but he will thrive where academic, scholarly, artistic, musical, cultural, detailed, or numerical skills are needed.

The Peaceful Phlegmatic (especially if his secondary personality is Sanguine) should not be in business for himself as he is most apt to be undisciplined, indecisive, procrastinating, and poor with money. He will function best in structured situations where the steps of progress are laid out and monitored, and where balance, objectivity, and managerial skills are desirable.

Go over your children's personalities and have them list occupations that would be naturals for them. Have them tell you why they would be successful in certain occupations and not in others. Get them thinking early in life about their future careers.

3. Arrange for them to talk with people in different professions. Reading about a variety of jobs is helpful, but conversing with those already in the field is better. When Marita was in high school I sent her for a week to my brother Ron to work and observe the radio business. When she saw what it entailed and how little glamour there was to being up at 4:30 in the morning, she lost interest. Seeing (and working!) is believing.

Throughout our children's lives we have entertained in our home a whole series of Christian speakers, authors, pastors, and missionaries from this country and abroad. We always included the children in the conversation and encouraged them to ask questions. Giving to missions is only a matter of money until you meet a missionary and find out what they really do.

4. Listen to your children's ideas and don't say, "That's a stupid idea. You'll never make any money that way." In the last year, as I have been doing a message called "Silver Boxes" encouraging all of us to encourage everyone else, I have told how my father could have been a great writer if he'd been encouraged. I mention that Fred's mother wanted to be an opera singer but her

parents told her she didn't have enough talent. As I tell these stories, people begin to cry and later come up to tell me of the dreams they once had that their parents ridiculed. So many of them never became what they could have been because they were discouraged by people whose opinions they respected.

Don't be a wet blanket on your child's dreams. Let him explore possibilities. When Randy [my oldest grandson] was little he told me he would be a speaker like me. Later he said he wanted to be a fireman. I asked, "Didn't you say you wanted to be a speaker?" Quickly he recouped, "I'll speak on fires." Now at ten he wants to be a doctor. With his Melancholy personality and exceptional ability in science, he may be heading for his future choice.

At six [my grandson] Jonathan has told me he's going to be a builder. As we took a walk through his neighborhood where several new houses are being built, he showed me many structural details that he had learned from his parents on previous tours. "Do you see how those front windows aren't even, Grammie? When I build houses I'm going to measure the windows." Since Jonathan is Sanguine, he will probably not measure anything, but I encouraged him in becoming a builder since that's where his thinking is today.

Listen to their dreams, let them imagine what they might be, and don't discourage their ideas no matter how ridiculous they might sound to you.

5. Help them choose the right courses to prepare them for future possibilities. With our hectic schedules today and with many working mothers, it's much easier to let our children take what they want in high school than to go over the lists and discuss what they would

need for certain colleges or occupations; yet the neglect of family participation in course selection can have a negative result. How sad it would be for your child to want to go to a certain college or vocational school only to find he is missing a key course for admission.

Don't leave the choices up to the high school whose job it is to get the right number of students into rooms staffed by the available teachers. Surely, I don't mean school counselors have no value, but always remember that the child is yours, not theirs.

6. Seek God's will in their future. Taking human steps is important, but as Christian believers we must train our children to seek God's will in all of life's choices. If you have had a vital family prayer life this step will be automatic but if you have all been closet Christians, if you have a nonbelieving spouse, or if you are a single parent whose time has been consumed in a daily struggle for existence, you will need to begin with the teaching that God cares about every part of our lives. (RTC/136-139)

DOUBT

When the devil wants to lead us astray, he sends an attractive item to cast doubt on God's Word. "You won't really die." "God didn't mean that line for you." "His Word is for old people in the old days." "You're free to do your own thing." (AEW/56)

99

E

ENCOURAGEMENT

One night after giving my "Silver Boxes" message, a little boy with big bright eyes came up to me and said, "I want your little box to take home."

"You want my silver box?" I asked.

"Yes, I need to have it."

"I'm so sorry," I replied, "but I need to keep it with me to use when I give this message."

Tears came to his eyes and he said, "I really need your box."

"What would you do with it?"

"I'd put it on my dresser and look at it every day so I'd say nice words."

Suddenly I realized it was more important for him to have the box than for me to keep it. I remembered the verse, "To him who knoweth to do good and doeth it not, to him it is sin" (James 4:17, KJV).

As I leaned down and placed the box in his hand, he reached up, kissed me and whispered, "I'll always remember you."

Later I thought of the possible consequences if I had refused to give him my silver box. He could have gone away thinking, "She talks about giving out silver boxes but she wouldn't give one to me." He could have decided, "All adults are selfish. All speakers are phonies."

I don't know what that wistful little boy did with the box. Perhaps he'll keep it on his dresser for years and teach the lesson to his friends. Perhaps his mother will throw it away one day when she's on a cleaning binge. No matter what happens, I did what I know was right and it may make a difference in that child's life. (BOX)

❑   ❑   ❑

When I was a senior in college, I came home for Christmas vacation and anticipated a fun-filled fortnight with my two brothers. We were so excited to be together we volunteered to watch the store so that my mother and father could take their first day off in years. The day before my parents went to Boston, my father took me quietly aside to the little den behind the store. The room was so small that it held only a piano and a hide-a-bed couch. In fact, when you pulled the bed out it filled the room and you could sit on the foot of it and play the piano. Father reached behind the old upright and pulled out a cigar box. He opened it and showed me a little pile of newspaper articles. I had read so many Nancy Drew detective stories that I was excited and wide-eyed over the hidden box of clippings.

"What are they?" I asked.

Father replied seriously, "These are articles I've written and some letters to the editor that have been published."

As I began to read, I saw at the bottom of each neatly clipped article the name Walter Chapman, Esq. "Why didn't you tell me you'd done this?" I asked.

"Because I didn't want your mother to know. She's always told me that since I didn't have much education I shouldn't try to write. I wanted to run for some political office also, but she told me I shouldn't try. I guess she was afraid she'd be embarrassed if I lost. I just wanted to try for the fun of it. I figured I could write without her knowing it, and so I did. When each item would be printed, I'd cut it out and hide it in this box. I knew someday I'd show the box to someone, and it's you."

He watched me as I read over a few of the articles and when I looked up, his big blue eyes were moist. "I guess I tried for something too big this last time," he added.

"Did you write something else?"

"Yes, I sent into our denominational magazine to give some suggestions on how the national nominating committee could be selected more fairly. It's been three months since I sent it in. I guess I tried for something too big."

This was such a new side to my fun-loving father that I didn't quite know what to say, so I tried, "Maybe it'll still come."

"Maybe, but don't hold your breath." Father gave me a little smile and a wink and then closed the cigar box and tucked it into the space behind the piano.

The next morning our parents left on the bus to the Haverhill Depot where they took a train to Boston. Jim, Ron, and I ran the store, and I thought about the box. I'd never known my father liked to write. I didn't tell my brothers; it was a secret between Father and me. The Mystery of the Hidden Box.

Early that evening I looked out the store window and saw my mother get off the bus—alone. She crossed the Square and walked briskly through the store.

"Where's Dad?" we asked together.

"Your father's dead," she said without a tear.

In disbelief we followed her to the kitchen where she told us they had been walking through the Park Street Subway Station in the midst of crowds of people when Father had fallen to the floor. A nurse bent over him, looked up at Mother and said simply, "He's dead."

Mother had stood by him stunned, not knowing what to do as people tripped over him in their rush in the subway. A priest said, "I'll call the police," and disappeared. Mother straddled Dad's body for about an hour. Finally an ambulance came and took them both to the city morgue where Mother had to go through his pockets and remove his watch. She'd come back on the train alone and then home on the local bus. Mother told us the shocking tale without shedding a tear. Not showing emotion had always been a matter of discipline and pride for her. We didn't cry either and we took turns waiting on the customers.

One steady patron asked, "Where's the old man tonight?"

"He's dead," I replied.

"Oh, too bad," and he left.

I'd not thought of him as the old man, and I was hurt at the question, but he was seventy-three and Mother was only fifty-three. He'd always been healthy and happy and he'd cared for frail mother without complaint, but now he was gone. No more whistling, no more singing hymns while stocking shelves; the Old Man was gone.

On the morning of the funeral, I sat at the table in the store opening sympathy cards and pasting them in a scrapbook when I noticed the church magazine in the pile. Normally I would never have opened what I viewed as a dull religious publication, but just maybe that secret article might be there — and it was.

I took the magazine to the little den, shut the door, and burst into tears. I'd been brave, but seeing Dad's bold recommendations to the national convention in print was more than I could bear. I read and cried and then I read again. I pulled out the box from behind the piano and under the clippings I found a two-page letter to my father from Henry Cabot Lodge, Sr., thanking him for his campaign suggestions.

I didn't tell anyone about my box; it remained a secret until we closed the store two years later and moved in with Grandma leaving the piano behind. I gave my last look to the empty kitchen with the old black stove standing staunchly alone while the bottle of kerosene gurgled loudly in the corner. I went quietly to the den, and as if in some religious rite, I reached behind the old piano where I'd practiced lessons and played hymns on Sunday evenings and pulled out *the box*.

Father left me no money, but he left me the box. He had little education and no degrees, but he gave me and my brothers a love for the English language, a thirst for politics, and an ability to write. Who knows what Father could have done with just a little encouragement?

Today as I stand in my study and look at Dad's article there on the wall matted in blue next to his picture smiling down at me and reread the letter from Lodge framed with his picture just below Father's, I realize how close I came to knowing none of this. How grateful I am that Father chose that day to reach behind the piano and pull out the box.

I'll never know what Walter Chapman, Esquire, could have been. Was there a great American novel inside him or at least a weekly column for the *Haverhill Gazette?* Could his charm and sense of humor have brought him political acclaim? — or could he at least have been the mayor of Haverhill?

How many of us as wives hold down our husband's aspirations, stifle a little bud of genius that's longing to burst forth? Why? Because we're afraid if he fails, we'll be embarrassed. How many are daunted by lack of degrees and don't dare to have their reach exceed their grasp?

Oh God, let us encourage one another unto good works (Hebrews 10:24-25). (YPT/210-213)

□　　□　　□

In one rare evening of genuine disclosure Fred's mother told me of her disappointments. "I never could please my father no matter how hard I tried, and I did my best to make my mother the queen she really wanted to be." I encouraged her to tell me how she really felt, and she shared one heart-breaking story.

She was in love with a young man while at Cornell and they had talked of marriage. Her mother disapproved because she felt he did not come from an important or wealthy enough family. After college they went in separate directions for the summer, and he was to call her in the fall. She never heard from him again.

105

At the mention of this fact, this beautiful woman burst into tears, and I thought the sad story was over. I'd never seen her let down her guard before, and I felt so sorry for how this rejection still bothered her. As I sat quietly, wondering what I should say, she looked up and continued. "That's not the end of it. I went to a party just a few years ago and there he was. I found out he was a successful lawyer, and then I asked that question, 'Why didn't you ever call me?' 'Oh, I called all right,' he replied. 'I talked to your mother on the telephone, and she told me that you were engaged to another man, that you didn't love me, and that you'd asked her to tell me never to call again.'"

Mother's ample frame shook as she sobbed out these last words. I knelt beside her and felt a warmth and compassion for her I'd never known before. How seldom we sense what's stored up inside a person just waiting for a quiet moment, a nonthreatening situation to be set free. My heart was broken with hers as she confessed, "I never felt right about Mother, but I didn't know why. I felt guilty because I couldn't love her enough, so I waited on her like a slave to ease my conscience. I tried to become what she wanted me to be, and I'll never know what I might have been."

"Was there anything you really wanted to be?" I asked. "An opera singer," she answered quickly. "I wanted to study music, but my parents felt that was a waste of time, that I'd make more money in the millinery business. But I was in one show in college, and I had the lead."

She got up quickly, went to a closet and pulled out a box of old pictures. She showed me a large photo of a stage setting with the cast posed for review. "There I am." She pointed proudly to a confident and beautiful young girl seated on an ornate chair, center stage, the obvious star of the show.

I'd not known of her operatic ambitions before, and I shared how I loved the theatre and had wanted to be an actress until my drama teacher told me I was much better at directing others. At the end of this memorable and meaningful evening, Mother gave me the picture of her on stage in her one starring role, and I treasure this memory of what might have been.

We'll never know what this talented, creative woman could have become had she been allowed to pursue her natural aims and abilities instead of being brought up to play the role of "perfect daughter." Suppressed ambitions never die; they wait inside for some moment of possible expression in the future.

Mother Littauer is now eighty-five years old, and her conscious mind is no longer functioning correctly. When Fred and I visited recently she had a peaceful expression on her face although she didn't seem to know who we were. When I talked with the nurse who cares for her, she said, "It's the strangest thing. She can't talk at all, but she sings opera each day and practices her scales."

How many of us have a suppressed opera, an imagined painting, a possible poem, the plot for a novel, the potential for a political career, or a thwarted adventure locked inside of us waiting for that magic key to set us free? Are you ready to sing a song in the spring? Perhaps like the Song of Solomon?

> *Arise, my darling,*
> *my beautiful one, and come with me.*
> *See! The winter is past;*

the rains are over and gone.
Flowers appear on the earth;
the season of singing has come.
—*Song of Songs 2:10-12,* NIV

You were made for such a time as this.
(YPT/213-216)

EYES

Watch for possible signs of hidden sadness in the eyes of busy people. (GAD/59)

□   □   □

It is not uncommon for a person who has suffered trauma as a child to reflect that residual hurt in her eyes. The most frequent type of look we see is:

Pained Eyes. This person may presently be going through a very painful, seemingly hopeless or traumatic time of life with a load that seems too big a burden to bear. On the other hand, she may have endured a sexual victimization, either known or suppressed, that has left deep wounds which have not yet been healed. We frequently see pained eyes at conferences when women come up after a session to ask questions. Recognizing this enables us to quickly get beyond the "presenting problem" to the "real problem," thereby helping them to focus on the source of their hurts, rather than on the symptom. Pained eyes in a woman who is also very much overweight has proven to be, in our experience, an indication of one who is bearing the burden of sexual abuse.

Dead Eyes. This is the look of a person who has already given up hope. She is resigned to live forever with seemingly desperate circumstances. Often, this person has no true sense of why she feels the way she does, why life seems so hopeless. Even the Christian, who intellectually understands the blessed hope that she has in Jesus, will be incapable of internalizing that truth to reflect the joy to which she is entitled. It will be difficult for her to accept the fact that Jesus can, and will, heal her of the deep, deep pain that is the result of this cavalier defilement of her body as a child. Often this person will have been the victim of long-term sadistic penetration, causing her emotions to die and leaving her without feelings.

Frightened Eyes. This person has probably suffered an attack trauma. She might have been raped at any age, as an adult or as a child. This assault on her mind and body was such a shock that the frightened look is evidence of an understandable fear of a recurrence at any time without warning. She is always on guard, looking for an escape, almost expecting to be victimized again. This intense fear of re-attack, even when it is unknown or unnamed, frequently leads to phobias, often to agoraphobia . . . fear of the outside world.

Eyes are the mirror of the soul. Sparkle reflects joy. Serenity reflects inner peace. Conversely, sexual trauma is reflected by pain, deadness and fear. (FYM/154-156)

F

FAMILY

In today's fast-paced society and frequent moves, we often lose the sense of family so vital in our own feelings of self-worth. I visited with a man who drove us to the airport recently. He called himself a "Louisiana Red-necked Baptist" and when talking of teen problems in his church, he said, "A lot of the trouble comes from our not spending time with our relatives and understanding the sense of tradition and family values. My mother didn't have to explain why we shouldn't do things, she'd just say, 'Our family doesn't do that.' We knew there was family pride at stake and we wouldn't do anything that would bring shame on the family name."

As he said this I realized that in my childhood I had been instilled with the same attitude. I never wanted to hurt my mother or disappoint my father. "Our family doesn't do that." Could we restore some of this sense of family if we visited with the cousins, aunts and uncles, and grandparents? While cousins seldom become best friends, knowing them and the other relatives gives our children a better sense of their heritage, a sense of belonging. (RTC/151)

□   □   □

What can you do if the relatives all live far away?

How can you keep the children in contact even under geographically distant conditions? If possible, plan special summer excursions to "go back home," to see the farm or visit the places where Mommy played. Make those trips special by preparing your children with stories and photos of you and the places you'll be visiting. And when the children are old enough let them visit other family members by themselves. These times with Grandma and Grandpa or aunts or cousins can be especially memorable if the child is the only one visiting. It could become a "rite of passage" by allowing each child to make a trip to Grammie's for their tenth birthday. (RTC/154)

□   □   □

My mother, "Grammie Chapman," lived with Lauren for three years before she died. The older boys, Randy and Jonathan, got to know "Grammie" and I was called "Other Grammie." My mother read stories to the boys and was always available in her rocking chair to hold one in her lap. Even though Bryan never knew her, he will still be able to touch base with his roots for while Grammie was still alive, Lauren did an intimate interview with her. She set up the video camera and started asking Grammie questions about her childhood and where she grew up. At first she was nervous, but once she got going on those old tales, she forgot all about the camera and captivated us all for several hours telling stories about my father that I didn't even know. This was a rare and tender time and now we have this memorable tape that will help the great-grandchildren "know" Grammie Chapman and have a better understanding of who they are and where they came from. (RTC/155)

Relatives help our children realize their roots, but they can also fill another important role. They can be a role model for our children. Parental love and encouragement is vital but other adults who are close to our children, who care about them, are also important to give them a balanced setting on which to form their views. (RTC/155)

FAVORITE STORIES

Many of you men allow more time for choosing a new car than you spend in selecting a wife. At the dealership you make sure the seats are well-padded, the steering wheel works, and the tires are properly inflated. But when you choose a bride, you soon see that her seat is over-stuffed, she refuses to be steered in any direction, and her wheels seem to be going around in circles.

If your lifelong dream is to own a long black Cadillac, you do not run out and buy a chubby little red Volkswagen and then take it home and bang it, stretch it, repaint it, and try to make it into a long, sleek, black Cadillac. Yet that is what many of you did in choosing a wife. You wanted a long black Cadillac but you married a chubby little red Volkswagen, and you've spent the last twenty years trying to beat it, pull it, and remake it into a black Cadillac.

Unfortunately, we just can't remake each other; we must accept each other as we are and not try to construct a new image of what the perfect mate should be. So, men, if you wanted a Cadillac with class and you got a Volkswagen with dents, accept her as she is. Ladies, if you thought you were getting a charging Cougar but ended up with a powerless Pinto, thank God you've got anything in the garage; and drive it gently. (AEW/77)

□   □   □

I always enjoyed plunking a whole bunch of cold, green grapes beside me and plucking off whatever one appealed to me. Until I married Fred, I didn't know there were "Grape Rules." I didn't know each simple pleasure in life had a so-called right way. Fred first brought up the Grape Rule as I was sitting on the patio outside our cottage at Cambridge Beaches in Bermuda, looking out to sea and absent-mindedly pulling grapes off a large bunch. I didn't realize Fred was analyzing my unsystematic eating of the fruit until he asked, "Do you like grapes?"

"Oh, I love grapes!"

"Then I assume you'd like to know how to eat them correctly?"

On that I snapped out of my romantic reveries and asked a question that subsequently became a part of a regular routine: "What did I do wrong?"

"It's not that you're doing it *wrong;* you're just *not* doing it right." I couldn't see that there was much of a difference, but I phrased it his way.

"What am I not doing right?"

"Anyone knows that to eat grapes properly, you cut off a little bunch at a time, like this."

Fred pulled out his nail clippers and snipped off a small cluster of grapes, which he set before me.

As he stood smugly staring down at me, I asked,

"Does this make them taste better?"

"It's not for taste. It's so the large bunch will keep its looks longer. The way *you* eat them—just grabbing grapes here and there—leaves the bunch a wreck. Look at what you've done to it! See all those tiny bare stems, sticking up all over the place? They ruin the shape of the whole bunch." I glanced around the secluded patio to see if there were some hidden group of grape judges waiting to enter my bunch in a contest, but seeing none, I said, "Who cares?"

I had not yet learned that "Who cares?" was not a statement to make to Fred, because it caused him to turn red and sigh with hopelessness, "I care, and that should be enough." (PPL/13-15)

◻ ◻ ◻

Last Christmas Aunt Marita gave her nephews Randy and Jonathan a hamster named Ginger. Each boy was constantly opening the cage to see if Ginger was still alive, and often they would lose interest in her monotonous trip round and round on the exercise wheel and forget to shut the gate. Ginger, being bright, adventurous and always hungry would run away and look for food. One day Lauren opened the trash compactor to drop in an empty cereal box and screamed when she saw little beady eyes looking up from the darkness. It was Ginger happily munching on stale crackers and missing death by a moment. Had Lauren turned the key without looking, little Ginger would have been as flat as a fur mitten.

From then on each time Ginger was missing, the boys would go to the trash compactor and there she would be, bright-eyed and bingeing.

One night I called on the phone and Randy, Jr., said, "Have you heard the bad news? Ginger is dead." I could picture her flattened out among the boxes and cans, but Randy explained, "She died in her cage. I went to play with her and she was dead." He then delivered a fitting eulogy and gave me the details. In his Melancholy way he told me how he and his father had found a little box in the garage, lined it with paper towels, wrapped poor Ginger in tissue paper, taken the box to a far corner of the back yard and buried her. "We had a funeral," he explained. "We'll always remember poor dead Ginger."

I was close to tears over his mournful musings of the memory of the hamster. When little Jonathan got on the phone, I said sadly, "I hear Ginger died."

He replied, "Yup, she's dead all right."

"Did you have a nice funeral for her?" I asked, giving him an opportunity to share his version of the tragedy.

"No, we didn't have any funeral; we just dumped her in an old box with clowns on it, stuck her in a hole in the ground, threw some dirt over her, and that's the end of Ginger."

"Will you get a new one?" I asked.

"Well, we might get another one, but if that one dies too then it's bye-bye hamsters!"

I had to laugh over his Sanguine dismissal of Ginger's death as just one more event in a busy day while his Melancholy brother was in mourning. (YPT/21-22)

□   □   □

One Sanguine who went to the Cotton Bowl for the New Year's game wanted to make sure she wouldn't get lost. She wrote down "Bus #104" on the back of an envelope so she would know which bus was hers when she returned. What she had not anticipated was that there were hundreds of buses all lined up and she had no idea which one was #104. "I would have been there yet," she exclaimed in typical Sanguine exaggeration, "if a friend hadn't found me gasping from the exhaust fumes and led me to Bus #104." (YPT/40)

□   □   □

An adorable Sanguine girl told me that her husband brought home a client for dinner. As she was preparing the meal she discovered she was missing a key ingredient. She didn't want her Melancholy husband to know since he constantly criticized her lack of organization, so she tiptoed to the front door. As she looked out she saw the client's car was behind hers in the driveway and she would have to go ask him to move it. But wait! There were his keys on the table so why not quietly take his car? She parked in the large lot outside the supermarket and when she came out she not only didn't know where she'd parked, she didn't have any idea what kind of a car it was. All she could remember was that there was a letter on the front seat and the only reason she recalled that was because she'd read it! She pushed her cart up and down lanes peering into each car looking for the letter which she ultimately found. She got home safely and no one ever needed to know, but in typical Sanguine fashion when there was a long pause in the business conversation, she felt led to entertain the client with her escapade of taking his car without permission and reading his letter. Much to her surprise he didn't find it humorous, and her husband was both humiliated and incensed. "Everyone else I told it to thought it was hilarious. I don't know what's the matter with them!" (YPT/40-41)

□   □   □

A Sanguine receptionist came out after work and her '67 Gold Dodge was gone. She called the police, filled out all the forms and asked the policeman to drive her home. When they pulled into the driveway the man asked, "Do you have two '67 Gold Dodges?"

"No, why?"

"Because there's one sitting here in front of us."

She looked up in wide-eyed surprise.

"Oh, I guess I forgot. My girlfriend drove me to work this morning." (YPT/41)

□   □   □

A girl from Fairbanks, Alaska, sent me this story after I spoke there in September of '85.

I went to [the supermarket] for a few quick items, but as I walked the aisles I decided I might as well shop. By the time I wandered the aisles (with payday's bulk in my purse), I had a cart chockful of meals. I also had a 'reduced for winter' Boston fern drooping atop the edibles!

Through the checkout stand, $158 later, I pushed my laden cart into the parking lot. Adrenalin pumped as I went row by row, puzzling over why I couldn't remember *where I'd parked. Still puzzled, I pushed the cart (topped by my Boston fern) back towards the store.*

The outside of the store was being painted by a crew on a scaffolding. As I dodged their equipment with my unwieldy cart, I saw it—beneath their tarp sat my yellow 10-speed bike!

I had biked the five miles today! Now, as a newly single parent whose ex-husband was out of town . . . who was in the 'proud' stage, too proud to call on a friend . . . I began packing:

—groceries into boxes stacked on the back rack

—cord tying the Boston fern pot firmly atop the boxes

—four loaves of bread tied by their ends to the handle bars.

I rode all the way home on a bike that was ready to flip over at every little bump! My daughters saw me come up . . . looking like a gypsy caravan!

How did I feel? . . . How did they feel? Resourceful! Capable! Independent! (YPT/42)

□   □   □

My very favorite episode is the lady from Newport Beach who went shopping at the vast South Coast Plaza. When she came out of Bullock's her car was gone. After hunting around by herself, she called the security guard who drove her up and down each row in the entire set of parking lots. There was no question; they both agreed; the car had been stolen. She filled out the forms and later filed an insurance claim. When she received the money, she bought a bright new car and liked it even better than the first one. Later she received a phone call from Sears, "Hey lady, when are you going to come back and pick up your car that you left here a month ago for us to rotate the tires? If you don't come soon, we're going to charge you for storage!" (YPT/42)

☐   ☐   ☐

So that you Sanguine men won't think these stories leave you out, here's an episode from my favorite minister of music, Jim Lacy, after his move to Columbus, Ohio.

Sanguine Jim and Melancholy Sherri went to a church Christmas party. Since they were new in town and hadn't become acquainted, Sherri was a little nervous about making a good first impression. Jim had the map to the people's home on Angela Street and Sherri was comforted when a car with some friends she recognized honked as they drove by. Since Jim had a quick errand to run at the church, he dropped Sherri off at the curb where she joined some others who were heading into the party.

Being new to the church and trying to be as outgoing as possible, Sherri greeted the hostess at the door and drifted into the room full of chatting couples. She stood by herself and observed that the new guests were all bringing wedding presents. She wondered why they were bringing these to the church Christmas party, and when she asked, the hostess replied, "This is no church Christmas party. This is a wedding reception. Are you supposed to be here?"

Sherri was so embarrassed that she got her coat

and left just as Jim was driving up oblivious to the fact he'd dumped her out at the wrong party. While Jim laughed Sherri went into a depression. When they got to the right house down the street, Sherri made Jim go in and make sure first. She begged him not to tell a soul, but in true Sanguine fashion, Jim made a comedy act of the whole episode. He wrote me, "I told everyone including my *Sanguine choir!* What fun!" (YPT/43)

□   □   □

When we lived in New Haven, Connecticut, the city built a seven-story parking garage. One day before Christmas, I parked my car in this gray cement structure that looked somewhat like an open penitentiary, and went off to do my shopping. Sanguines, being circumstantial people with short memories, have difficulty in locating misplaced items, such as cars; and when I walked out of Macy's and faced this foreboding fortress, I had *no* idea where I'd left my car.

One good thing about a Sanguine woman is that she has a helpless look and can usually attract attention. True to Sanguine form, I stood staring up at the seven stories and wondered where I should start. A handsome young man walked by, noticed I was bewildered, holding an armload of bundles, and asked, "What's your trouble, honey?"

"I lost my car in this seven-story garage."

"What kind of a car is it?"

"Well, that's part of the problem. I don't know."

"You don't know what kind of a car you own?" he asked in disbelief.

"Well, we own two, and I don't know which one I drove today."

He thought for a minute and then said, "Let me see your keys, and I can narrow it down."

That was no easy request, because I had to set down all my packages and empty out my entire handbag on the curb before I found two sets of car keys. By this time, another man, seeing me on my knees in the gutter, asked, "What's the matter here?"

The first man said, "She's lost her car in the seven-story parking garage."

He asked the same question: "What kind of a car is it?"

"She doesn't know."

"She doesn't *know?* Then how can we ever find it?"

I explained, before they both gave up, "It's either a yellow convertible with black insides and red dials, or a large, navy blue car with matching velour seats."

They both shook their heads, picked up my packages, and led me off to the parking garage. As we searched seven stories, other helpful souls attached themselves to our group, and we became acquainted. By the time we found the yellow convertible with the license plate O FLO we were such good buddies, I wanted to start a club and be president.

I rushed right home, eager to tell Fred every detail of my marvelous moments of hide-and-seek in the garage. Fifteen beautiful minutes later when I concluded my story, I hoped he would say, "Wasn't that wonderful of all these men to help my little wife." But, no. He shook his head solemnly and sighed, "I am so embarrassed to be married to a woman so stupid as to lose her car in a seven-story parking garage."

I soon learned to save my stories for those who would appreciate my sense of humor. (PPL/29-30)

◻   ◻   ◻

One wedding I attended was conducted by a handsome pastor. He came out before the wedding, clipped on his mike, and announced the opening song. Suddenly a look of panic came over his face; he took off his mike, and he ran back and forth between the two pulpits searching through papers. The wedding march started, so he ran back to position, clipped on the mike, and gave a big smile to the audience. The service was charming and personal but with unusual vows. Suddenly he stopped and asked the couple to kneel for one minute of silent prayer. He instructed the congregation and the wedding party to bow their heads, close their eyes, and meditate. While they were doing as he asked, he quickly took off the mike, bolted out the side door, ran across the patio, and disappeared into his office. Instantly he emerged carrying a book, tiptoed back in place, clipped on his mike, took a deep breath, and said, "Amen." He then opened the book and proceeded to read the rest of the ceremony correctly. (The silent prayer kept most heads down, but naturally I peeked, and Fred clocked the trip at forty-seven seconds.) (PPL/101-102)

◻   ◻   ◻

The last Christmas we had with my little Phlegmatic mother was one to remember. Her Choleric sister Jean, my favorite aunt, came out to California bringing a special present for Mother from her friends at the church "gift shop." As Mother was carefully unwrapping the present in such a way as to preserve the paper for next year, Aunt Jean spoke up. "This is a very special present. Your friends made this by hand for you and you will love it." As Mother took a look, Aunt Jean continued, "That is an apron, made of unbleached muslin and edged in red bias binding." Cholerics somehow feel Phlegmatics are not bright enough to know an apron when they see one, muslin from satin, or red from green. "Written all over the apron in liquid embroidery are all your friends' names. See them right there. They all sat down and signed the apron so that every time you wear it you will think of them."

Mother quietly stated, "I won't wear this apron; it's too good to use."

"What do you mean you won't wear this apron! Do you think I'm going back to 'gift shop' and tell them that after all their time and effort you wouldn't even wear the apron!"

Lauren on the other side of Mother said firmly, "You *will* wear this apron. In fact right after Christmas dinner you will put it on to do the dishes."

As Mother folded it back up, Aunt Jean added, "I didn't drag this apron all the way out here on the plane from Massachusetts to have you refuse to wear it!"

Lauren affirmed to Aunt Jean, "She *will* wear it. I'll see to it."

Mother put the cover on the box and said softly, "I will not wear this apron." Lauren and Aunt Jean, two

Cholerics having trouble with their control, said in harmony, "You *will* wear that apron."

A month later when I was conducting a *Personality Plus* Conference in Dallas, Mother was sitting right in the front row. As I was speaking I wondered if I dared tell the story about Mother and the apron. I remember thinking, "Well, she's eighty-five. She can't hate me for too long." I took the big chance and went through the whole scene ending with, "And Mother said, 'I won't wear that apron.'"

Much to my absolute amazement, Phlegmatic Mother stood up, turned to the crowd and stated clearly, "And I didn't!" They loved her and gave her a rousing ovation.

Later when I commended her performance I told her, "You ought to be the speaker. I spoke all day and you got an ovation on one line." She gave a little Phlegmatic shrug and I could tell, in her terms, that she was "pleased as punch." (YPT/49-50)

FELLOWSHIP

Time is so valuable we cannot afford to waste it on purposeless chatter. In our family we now have five adult men: Father Fred; Fred; Lauren's husband, Randy; Marita's husband, Chuck; and Brenda's husband, Ken. (Brenda lived with us for many years and is like part of the family.) [When we all lived in the same town] Father Fred realized how little time he spent with the boys, so he scheduled a once-a-month men's night. He took them all out to a restaurant for dinner and led them in some structured conversation. As they shared their feelings about their childhoods, their careers, and their goals, they got to know each other. My husband looked forward to hosting times of true fellowship and he sensed a new love and understanding among the family men. (ITS/151)

FORGIVENESS

Few of us enjoy forgiving others because it implies that what they did wasn't so bad, when it really was! If we really forgive we might also forget the evidence, and what if we need it for proof in the future? Our minds function on such a selfish level that we don't like to let go of the bad examples of others. Not only do we not want to forgive, but we take pride in repeating the tales of others' grand mistakes because it shows we don't do any of these things ourselves. Obviously, if I have the discernment to see the error of your ways then I must be above suspicion myself.

I used to gather up Fred's faults with the fervor of a child picking berries. I had a whole shelf of overflowing baskets before the concept of forgiveness fell heavily upon me. To be spiritual I plucked out a few of Fred's faults and forgave them, but I didn't want to clear the whole shelf. Where would I go for future reference material? (AEW/91)

FRIENDSHIP

I realized a principle in getting along with people: We should give them what they desire and not be looking for them to fill our needs. (GAD/162)

G

GENTLENESS

Although the world tells us to be assertive, the Word tells us to be gentle. (AEW/101-102)

GOALS

We have all tried so hard to find happiness but have somehow missed the mark. While most of us are not hungry for food, many of us are starving for purpose and direction in life. Not only have we failed to find fulfillment as adults, but we have left our children without goals. (BBC/16)

□   □   □

An elegantly dressed lady came to me one day in Newport Beach, California, and said sadly, "I think I've raised a bum. I have a twenty-five-year-old son who goes surfing every day, and he seems depressed."

I asked her the obvious questions—where he lived, how he supported himself, how he got to the beach. "He lives with us in a big house up on the hill," she said. "We have plenty of room and I like to keep him around. I give him whatever money he needs, and he drives to the beach in the sports car we gave him for his birthday. He ought to be happy."

Why was her son depressed? He had everything he needed in life, but no goals. Why work when everything was handed to him? He had won the battle, but he wasn't enjoying the victory. (BBC/16)

☐   ☐   ☐

As we made plans for our first family meeting, Fred and I sat down seriously and began to map out our long-range objectives. Looking back we can now see the value in our goal-planning and in our giving ourselves a measuring stick by which to judge our performance as directors. We first came up with a definition of what our desires should be for a family. So often we don't realize we need a guideline, but when we have none, there's nothing by which we can check our decisions. The following statement of purpose has helped us, and many others, to focus on a family plan:

Our desire is to bring up well-adjusted children who will be able to function responsibly without us.

Our goal is not to reign forever but to abdicate gracefully at the right time. (RTC/110-111)

☐   ☐   ☐

As a parent my [goal] has been to train my children to be self-sufficient, to show them how much work it is to maintain a home, to teach all the children growing up that housework is a shared obligation, not a sole project for Mother, and then, most important of all, praise each one for what they've done, especially if it was beyond what they were assigned.

By following this plan, I have been able to raise children who are responsible adults who can get along without me. (RTC/113)

GUILT

What happens when we ignore God's clear warnings and follow *temptation* into *sin?* We instantly feel guilty. God has equipped us with a guilty conscience to help keep us in line. When we step off to the tune of our own drummer, guilt stops us in our tracks and we quickly try to involve someone else to dilute our own pressure. (AEW/57)

□   □   □

A psychiatrist told me that a large portion of people in mental hospitals today are there because they have a guilty conscience they can't release over some mistake they made many years ago. (OCP/66)

□   □   □

Is there a spiritual way to handle guilt? Yes, there is; I've used it.

First, we must divide our guilt in two categories: Ask God to bring to your mind the things you feel guilty about and write them down. Keep writing until you can't think of anything more. Now go back over the list. After each item ask yourself, "Do I feel guilty about this because I really am guilty? Are my emotions justified? Have

I really done something wrong?" Where the answer is "yes," put a checkmark.

Perhaps you are depressed by some guilt you know you could do something about. Look over your list and get moving.

How much of your guilt is unnecessary? Are people expecting more of you than you can handle? Are people pressuring you into positions you have no time for? Are people judging you according to their own narrow standards?

You can't please everyone. You can only do the best you know how to under the circumstances and not worry about what people think. Ask the Lord right now to remove all the guilt that has been put upon you by other people.

There is nothing we can do about changing our friends' behavior, but we can deal with unnecessary guilt in a spiritual way. When someone tries to make you feel guilty, thank him for the suggestion and tell him you will certainly give it serious consideration. If it has merit, think about it; if it does not, ask the Lord to quickly remove even the memory of the statement from you.

Before you go any further, make sure you have looked over those patchwork guilts that are covering up your joy. Then ask the Lord to fold them up and put them away in a distant closet. Believe Him when He says they are gone. Don't go hunting for them again. They're the Lord's property. And we have the promise in Hebrews 9:14 that He will make our consciences clean. (BBC/107-116)

H

HATRED

A young lady came to me with a tale of hostility toward her husband. As she poured out all his misdeeds, they seemed so trivial that I asked her when her feelings of hatred had started. She replied quickly, "I was mad at him before we even got married."

He had written her a letter instructing her to find a car for their honeymoon trip. She had answered that it was his responsibility to provide transportation, and besides, his family had three cars while hers had only one. He made it clear: "If you want to marry me, you had better find a car!" She found a car, but she vowed she would never forget his injustice.

She looked up at me with bitterness lining her face and said, "In case you don't believe me, I'll show you the letter he wrote." She reached into her handbag and pulled out a worn and tattered envelope that had moved from bag to bag for ten years. As she handed it to me, she said, "I always carry it with me so I won't forget."

Probably none of us has a letter like this in our handbag, but we may have one in our heads. How can God work in a heart hardened with hatred? How can we ever know joy when we are busy recording indelibly our partner's mistakes? (AEW/48)

HONESTY

Often we Christians feel exempt from worldly restrictions because we're doing it "for the Lord" who, if He happens to notice our little theft, will forgive us when He sees what a blessing we've been to the budget. (LFG/154)

□   □   □

God feels telling the truth is important and teaching our children to be honest is a necessity if we wish them to become adults pleasing to the Lord. (LFG/154)

HOPE

How often we say "the whole thing's on the rocks. It's over. There's no hope." Are you feeling on the rocks today? Look up to God as Jacob did in his wilderness, for wherever you are, this spot may be your gate to heaven. It's an awesome place; surely God is here. (LFG/75)

HOSPITALITY

One of our most successful parties was the night we arranged to have the Good Humor Ice Cream truck come to our driveway at 8 o'clock. As the bell clanged, all the surprised guests filed out to choose whatever flavors they wished and to stand in the street and eat ice cream. We do not need to have a large income or great culinary skills to entertain; we can invite Christian friends to our homes and have fellowship while eating ice cream outside. (AEW/45)

□   □   □

Hospitality doesn't depend on [the] size [of your home], but on spirit. (ITS/137)

□   □   □

The Bible tells us to use hospitality one to another without grudging (1 Peter 4:9). Peter tells us to open up our homes without complaining. How often I hear a woman bemoaning the fact that she has to have some people over. How much fun will these people have? How do I feel when a lady tells me she can't come to my seminar because she's been assigned to cook my dinner and it will take her all day? As she sighs, I wonder if I'm worth eight hours of preparation. Wouldn't it be better if she came to the sessions? We would then have a mutual subject for conversation while letting the "Colonel" do the cooking. (ITS/137)

□   □   □

The Bible says we should open our homes to strangers. Yes, get into the habit of entertaining even overnight. It's much easier to get out of the habit than it is to get into it. Feeding groups at a moment's notice is not easy but as you get in the habit, it can be fun. I always made sure to have staples on hand for certain basic dishes and when Fred let me know at five o'clock that a few friends were in town, I was able to put together an adequate meal—remembering that no one expects a gourmet treat, they just enjoy a simple meal at home.

As I was raising my children they always got excited about having company "overnight," whether it was their friends or strangers. They all knew they could bring home anyone who needed a place to stay and we have "thereby" entertained many "angels unaware." (ITS/138)

HUSBANDS

Our husbands are to be our number one friend in life. We are to put them first, care for them, and please them. This principle does not mean that we sit home like doormats waiting to be stepped on. It does not mean that we don't have an original thought of our own. It means that we put our husbands first—before our children, before our parents, before our friends, and before our activities. No one has ever thought of me as meek and mild, and yet I put Fred first. Men, for us to put you first and make our lives revolve around you, you've got to be something with some wit, some knowledge, some personality, some manners, and some style. How can we put you in your rightful position if you are dull, drab, dreary, selfish, conceited, and arrogant? Help us out, please! (AEW/72)

□　　□　　□

So many men feel that by downgrading and insulting their wives they are impressing others with how tolerant and competent they are in comparison with the poor dumb thing they have had to live with all these years.

Men, when you try to convince others of your

competence by cutting down your wife, what are you really saying? "I am an insecure man who hopes to cover up my inferiority complex by browbeating my wife into abject submission so you'll be impressed with my strength." How we want to flee from that type of a rude, insensitive brute who has to build his ego at the expense of others! (AEW/109)

□   □   □

Men, when you marry you are responsible to support your wife, to care for her, and to maintain the home. Are you keeping up with your bills or have you so overextended yourselves that she must work night and day to pay the rent? Have you mowed the lawn or is the grass so high that your backyard looks like a wild meadow?

While you men are to be our heads, do not misread this as meaning tyrants or dictators. You should use honest will in dealing with us and provide inspirational leadership. You are to be our guides, our reference material, and our spiritual leaders. You are to be our priests, providers, and protectors. (AEW/73)

□   □   □

Don't be discouraged, men, if you make all the improvements and she seems unwilling to respond. Years of hurt feelings can't be repaired overnight. You be the one to start. Show her that she comes first in your life, and she won't be able to resist you.

When your wife is doubtful of your love, she'll demand things.

When she knows you love her unconditionally, she won't care what else she owns.

When you are a loving husband you will produce a pleasing wife.

"Whatsoever a man soweth, that shall he also reap . . . Let us not be weary in well-doing, for in due season we shall reap if we faint not" (Galatians 6:7,9).

REMEMBER: If you want heaven at eleven start before seven! (AEW/139)

I

IMMATURITY

Our friend Lynn was sent to a town she did not like, and she vowed that she would not put up any curtains as long as her husband made her stay there. She explained to me, "If I put up curtains, he might think I was adjusting to my situation." They lived unhappily in the sight of all the neighbors for two years, until he ran off and married a girl with drapes! (AEW/41)

□   □   □

What is now called the "dependency personality" starts in childhood when a child is not taught responsibility, does not learn how to compete, and thinks that Mother will always sweep ahead, parting the Red Seas of life.

We parents have to realize that our goal is not to have our children cling to us forever, professing their need for protection, but to bring them up in such a way that they will be able to face life without us. (BBC/41)

□   □   □

When Marita went off to college she took everything from our house that wasn't nailed down. Her car was so full she couldn't shut the windows as she and her friend Peggy pulled out on a Sunday afternoon. They were going off to a Christian college specifically to take a course taught by our family friend, Dr. Henry Brandt. At 7:45 the next morning Marita called to say she was through with college and was coming home. I replied, "That has to be the shortest college career on record."

She explained that Dr. Brandt was not coming this term and so she was not going to stay.

"Don't they teach any other courses at that school?" I asked.

"I knew you'd be no help," she fumed.

"This will be a great opportunity for you to put the maturity lesson into practice," I said. "So find some other class and make the best of your situation."

At the end of the week Marita came home for a visit and brought me a note from Peggy.

"We want to show our parents that even though the class wasn't our favorite choice, we will make the best of it anyway." (AEW/42-43)

INDECISION

Indecision is a basic decision to never make another decision. By not offering clear opinions, you avoid specific responsibilities and escape from ever being to blame for family mistakes.

This passive attitude may keep [a husband] from getting an ulcer, but it is an abdication of his Scriptural position as the head of the household. When a man lets his wife assume authority, one of two things usually hap-

137

pens as the years go on. Either —

he feels henpecked and wants to leave,

or

she looks down at him in disgust and wants to throw him out. (AEW/121)

INTRODUCTIONS

The purpose of an introduction [of a speaker] is to "break down the middle wall of partition between us" (Ephesians 2:14). These brief moments should be prepared carefully to achieve this desired result, to "break down the wall" between the speaker and the audience. Think of yourself as the connecting link between the two, as a bridge from the mouth of the speaker to the mind of the hearer. (ITS/122)

J

JOURNALIZING

What good does journalizing do me? Your writing becomes a personal record of your inner life. As you look back over your thoughts, you will remember how you felt and you will see patterns of behavior which may need to be changed. (ITS/75)

□   □   □

David was a master journalizer and his psalms are ours today because he took the time to write down his feelings. He talked to God in a personal way and his thoughts then are so like ours today. (ITS/76)

□   □   □

By journalizing you devise a plan, you commit your feelings to paper each day. As you review these, you form a mental picture of what your inner life was like at that moment.

So to journalize is to think, planning today to make mental pictures for the future. (ITS/78)

□   □   □

Make journalizing work for you. Make a note anytime you feel emotions welling up inside in response to something you are reading. It may be very significant, for *our emotions remember what our mind has forgotten.* (FYM/11)

L

LEADERSHIP

To be a leader, by definition, a person must be in front, must march ahead of the others. No matter how bright or right a person may be, he can't be a leader if no one else chooses to follow. The elusive quality of leadership is the ability to inspire others to want to do your will. Without this appeal, the intentional leader is a captain without a ship, a king without a country. (PPO/10)

□   □   □

When it's time to choose the new leader, management frequently reaches for the one who has no enemies. (PPL/77)

□   □   □

In our country we have longed for leadership, we've wanted a king, and we have often been willing to accept a lack of managerial skills or even mediocre performance if we could have a regal leader to inspire hopes beyond belief, to lead us toward an impossible dream. (PPO/10)

□   □   □

In 1 Timothy 3:12 Paul tells us that a Christian leader should have only one wife and be able to manage his children and his family well. Each one of us believers is a Christian leader in some sphere of life—at work, at school, at the club. In many places we go we may be the only true believer in the group. As people begin to identify us as Christians, how important it is that we manage our children well! (AEW/70)

□   □   □

The ABCs of leadership give us some simple guidelines. Have the:

Attitude of a servant

Bearing of a queen [or king]

Clothing of a leader. (ITS/110)

□   □   □

So few leaders take the time or effort to find out what the purpose of the flock is and bumble through half the year before finding out no one knows where they're going. If there is no true goal, either think one up or disband the group. (ITS/126)

□   □   □

The big secret in confident leadership is in being prepared. There is no way you can be consistent in conducting your meetings if you run in at the last minute and try to pull the thing together. We had a pastor once who often came to the Wednesday night Bible study with no idea of what he was going to do. When he was prepared he would walk in briskly, go immediately to the pulpit and present an exciting program. On those nights when he would come in casually and shake hands with every person in an aisle seat, I knew he wasn't ready and prayed the Holy Spirit would reveal a three-point outline to him as he wandered through the church.

Preparation is essential for your own self-confidence and for the comfort of the people. When you are agitated, they get nervous. (ITS/127)

◻   ◻   ◻

In the thirty years I have been involved with all types of club, church and organizational work, I have found that when the presiding officer leads with loving authority, the group will follow with respect. But if she is insecure, nervous, and confused they will swoop in upon her as vultures. If you know the purpose of your position, have a clear goal for the year, have done your homework, arrive early and prepared, you will preside with confidence. (ITS/132)

◻   ◻   ◻

One of the major reasons why we, as the American public, become disillusioned with our leaders is that we feel, way down inside, that there is a perfect president, a perfect pastor, a perfect person. The most practical-minded businessman still has fairy-tale ideas about the possibility that the next president will have the "right stuff."

We practice this wish-fulfillment theory in our

choice of mates, friends, business associates, and pastors, and carry it over to our expectations of our children. We want them all to exhibit every strength we have projected on them and no matter how intelligent we may be, we are still shocked when our choice, or our flesh and blood, fails us.

Until we have a concept of the four basic personalities, we are constantly open to disappointment in others; but once we understand that each person comes pre-packaged, with sets of strengths and weaknesses, we can anticipate both their victories and their failures and not be surprised. We have a measuring stick we can use that may be able to predict some future reactions and behavior patterns. (PPO/120)

LISTENING

No one listens to anyone any more; they're all too busy, so if we just listen, we become a devoted friend. Everywhere I go, on planes, in lines, in the ladies room, I find people who give me their buckets of burdens. I don't have to make up case histories, I only have to listen. They can sense that I care and they talk. Sometimes a stranger after pouring out a whole life upon me will suddenly say, "I don't know why I told you all this." She had to tell it to someone and I was there. (ITS/168)

LONELINESS

Psychologists have told us for years that our greatest human desire, after self-preservation, is to be needed. We desperately want someone who needs us. We can be told convincingly that we will be happier alone, but underneath we want someone who cares. (OCP/28)

LOVE

If you've been looking for God in a few wrong places, perhaps you should review the commandments and see if you've been playing in the gray area—not too bad but not quite in line with God's laws. With God it's "All or nothing at all." Half a love isn't enough for him. (LFG/158)

□   □   □

Even though we all preach unconditional love, we have trouble really living it. We get along fine with those who agree with us and live according to our standards but it's difficult not to judge the sinner and condemn the fallen. If we know more than ten verses by heart we feel called upon to stand with Moses and discern with Solomon. We tend to say, "I love you if . . .". and "I'll accept you when . . . ." (ITS/172)

M

MARRIAGE

Because of our differences in background we had divergent expectations. I thought marriage would be fun, but Fred wanted me to get down to business. When we returned from our honeymoon, Fred put me on a training program. He wanted me to be the perfect wife, and he worked to teach me how to walk, talk, look, and cook. I thought I knew enough already. I quietly rebelled at his instructions. He persevered and felt that I should be grateful to be so well-trained. (AEW/14)

□   □   □

When Fred and I first wrote the material on marriage for an adult Sunday school course, we were not Bible scholars and we had not even read one book on marriage, and yet our home had been changed by applying scriptural truths to our lives. We wanted to share the excitement of Christian principles with others, and so we began to study. Armed with several Bibles, a concordance, and a topical Bible, we set out on a search to show others the standards of the Scripture in practical terms.

The first advice on marriage in the Bible is given in Genesis 2:24, where God says, "Therefore shall a man leave his father and his mother and shall cleave unto his wife, and they shall become one flesh." When we marry we are to set up a new unit of living; we are to leave our parents and start a separate entity. If we are not economically or emotionally ready to leave home, there is little hope for a mature marriage. God gave us sound advice, and when we ignore it we open ourselves for heartache. (AEW/69)

□   □   □

No matter what hedonistic headlines tell you about it being okay if you stray, remember that God's Word, the only stable psychology manual available, says don't stray—stay. If you cared enough to marry her, live with her. (AEW/107)

□   □   □

When you're old enough to leave [your parents], leave. And then cleave, latch onto one another, cling tightly, merge together, become one. Many of the secular articles on marriage tell us to keep our own identity, our own separate friends, and our own bank accounts, and to go our own ways, not getting dependent on one another or becoming too close. Then why get married at all? God tells us to unite and become as one. (AEW/114)

□   □   □

Marriage should not be an institution you flee to when you get caught, but a uniting of two mature adults who are in love and excited about committing their lives to each other "till death do us part." That expression may sound old-fashioned, but marriage based on any other reason but love and commitment will be doomed to failure. (OCP/69)

MASKS OF PERSONALITY

Those of us who don't know who we are usually have changed our personality in the past because of some circumstances that showed we were not acceptable as we were. The little Perfect Melancholy girl wants to please Popular father. Every time she goes to him with problems, he cheers her up by saying, "It's no big deal. Lighten up. You're always too serious. Why can't you be fun like your sister Suzy? See how happy she is? See how she tells stories and entertains her many friends? You'd be a lot better off if you could just try to be like Suzy."

The child, a serious and thoughtful little girl, analyzes what's been said. She wants to please her fun-loving father and be popular like Suzy, and so without knowing what she's doing to her future self-worth, she puts on a Popular Sanguine mask and tries to be like Suzy. This act may please her father and may fool many people, but when I face this lady at forty trying desperately to maintain a lighthearted approach to life, swinging frequently from loud laughter to outbursts of tears, depressed at her lack of serious achievement, and totally at a loss as to who she is, I see the results of a mask put on to please a parent. (RTC/83)

□   □   □

When we play God with other people's personalities, especially our children's and our mates', we may change the original behavior, but what do we have on our hands? We have a mongrel, a phony personality, one that is forced to function in weaknesses and not in strengths. It's like breeding a Schnauzer with a poodle. It's a cute little thing, but what is it? (PPO/113)

□ □ □

Some masks are initially put on for self-defense. A child who is beaten or sexually molested often changes his or her personality in the mistaken belief that it is this nature that brings on the abuse. "If only I weren't like this, he wouldn't hurt me." The most frequent mask put on for this reason is the Perfect Melancholy one. "I will do everything right. Then I won't have these problems." Even if the child was born with a perfectionistic nature, playing this role leads to emotional chaos, for no matter how hard the child tries, the behavior doesn't remove the abuse. (RTC/86)

□ □ □

People who have been abused, controlled or manipulated often put on the Melancholy mask of pain and perfection or give up by putting on the Phlegmatic mask of peace at any price. This last mask is often worn by a Powerful Choleric who has been beaten down and who has wrapped himself or herself in a cloak of indifference. "Who cares anyway? What does it matter? I'll just let them have their way." Powerful Choleric persons want to control but if they sense they can't win, they refuse to play the game. They put on a mask of peace and tune out on at least part of life.

The Powerful Choleric mask of control is donned

by any of the other personalities who don't want to be in charge but who are pushed into a parenting role at a young age. This can be caused by an alcoholic parent who is irresponsible, a set of working parents who put responsibility on one child to oversee the others, a home where drugs rob the children of consistent and loving discipline, or by parents who are extremely immature. Whenever the child says to himself or herself, "This family is not going to make it if I don't take charge," the child is assuming a demanding role and becoming a little controller. This mask of premature power becomes confusing to the child in charge and causes swings of passive-aggressive behavior as he grows up. (FYM/41)

◻   ◻   ◻

Two generalities that I have observed in those wearing masks are: (1) They have a tremendous well of suppressed anger which can erupt at anytime without logical explanation; and (2) they are frequently exhausted and often looking for some medication to pep them up.

The anger was deposited in them when they first put on their mask. An abused little girl couldn't fight back and any expressed anger was an invitation for more punishment. She learned to hide her anger and not let it show. A parent made a child be something contrary to his inborn nature showing him in his heart that he was not acceptable as he was. This feeling of rejection caused anger but because he couldn't express it openly he pushed it down inside. Much adult anger comes from childhood hurts and rejections that have never been recognized.

The exhaustion comes from the amount of energy

it takes to play an unnatural role. If you've ever been in a play or a pageant and had to act a part that wasn't you (and hoped you'd say the right lines at the appropriate time), you know the pressure you were feeling. Even if you loved acting, your pulse rate increased and your adrenalin raced and when you went to get up the next morning you were exhausted. When you suppress your own natural emotions and put on a mask, you are acting twenty-four hours a day, seven days a week. No wonder you are exhausted! (RTC/90)

□　　□　　□

The Sanguine mask of popularity is not so common as the mask of pain, the mask of peace at all costs, or the mask of control, but it is often found in Christian homes where the family must exude the joy of the Lord at all times no matter how they really feel. "Don't come out until you have a smile on your face. A real Christian is always happy. Be ye joyful!"

A child who is assigned to cheer up an ailing parent, who is expected to be adorable and witty like her sister or who is forced into an up-front role which does not fit her natural personality may put on the mask of attempted popularity to please a parent. (FYM/43)

MATURITY

According to the dictionary, maturity is "a growing up, a completeness, a ripening, a full development." We all feel that we've grown up and that each one of us has completed something. A few of us may be overripe and some are too fully developed. A better way to check our maturity is to ask, "Have we learned to *accept responsibility* and *adjust to our situations?*"

When God directed our family to leave Connecticut, where we had lived for thirteen years, to move into the desert of California, I was brokenhearted. I was very new in my Christian faith and I had not experienced God's firm direction and constant care for me. All I could see was the leaving of a secure situation for a frightening future. I didn't know enough about the Bible to realize that when God wanted to teach people lessons, He often sent them to deserts. As I sat sadly in San Bernardino studying God's Word, I found Paul's verse on maturity in Philippians 4:11: *"I have learned, in whatsoever state I am, therewith to be content."*

Did this mean that I should be content in the State of California? Yes. Could I leave lush, green Connecticut with its assets and be happy in the desert of California with its uncertainties? Paul said that he had to learn to be content. It didn't come easily. I determined to learn to be content in California. That agreement with God was my first step in growing up. I must learn in whatever state I am to be content. (AEW/36)

□   □   □

Maturity comes when we are able to accept our present position in life and adjust to our situation with gratitude. We need to praise the Lord anyhow! (BBC/71)

MELANCHOLIES/PERFECTS

Where the Sanguine is an extrovert, the

Melancholy is an introvert. Where the Sanguine loves to talk and throw everything out in the open, the Melancholy is deep, quiet, and thoughtful. Where the Sanguine views life through rose-colored glasses, the Melancholy is born with a pessimistic nature, which makes him foresee problems before they happen and count the cost before he builds. The Melancholy always wants to get to the heart of the matter. He doesn't take things at face value, but digs into the inner truths. (PPL/41)

□   □   □

The Melancholies are the most talented and creative of them all. They may be artistic, musical, philosophical, poetic, literary. They appreciate gifted people, admire geniuses, and admit an occasional tear of emotion. They are moved by the greats of all mediums, and they marvel at the wonders of nature. They sink into symphonies and get wired on their woofers. The more Melancholy they are, the more stereo components they need. (PPL/44)

□   □   □

The Melancholies are assets on committees because they ask questions about the details overlooked by the Sanguines, such as *Can we afford this project? How much will it cost to rent the hall? How many people do you think will come? How much are you going to charge? Is there a demand for this activity? Do you realize the dates you've chosen are on Easter weekend?* Without Melancholy balance, many committees would go wild with enthusiasm without counting the cost. (PPL/47)

□　□　□

A young girl told me she was helping a lady clean her house as an after-school job. She finished her work and returned all the bottles to the cabinet. As she turned to leave, the lady called her back to tell her she had not put things away properly. The girl gasped, as the lady showed her circles drawn on the shelf paper to indicate exactly where each can or bottle went—round for Ajax, oval for Windex, rectangle for detergent, big round for bleach. She placed everything on its own space and said, "When you keep things in perfect order, you can always put your hands on them quickly." (PPL/47)

□　□　□

A Melancholy pastor told me how as a child he kept all of his games in order, numbered each box and had a master list posted in his closet. He never lost so much as a puzzle piece in his whole childhood. When he had his own children and gave them his well-preserved games to play with, "They had all the parts messed up within a week. How could I have kept them perfect for all those years and see them wreck the whole system in less than a week?"

A Sanguine girl told me her Melancholy husband has rebuilt her closet three times in hopes he'll strike the right plan which will make her keep it neat. If only he knew the temperaments, he could save his time and money. No matter what plan he has, she'll still throw the shoes in a pile on the floor.

Another girl wrote, "My Melancholy husband keeps his side of the closet in perfect order with all of his pants folded exactly the same. You can imagine what my side looks like! He even gets bothered when I don't put the shampoo and creme rinse bottles back on the rack with the labels facing forward in perfect order! It took him six months to tell me this bothered him."

One Melancholy man kept a "mileage chart" on his shoes from the time he bought them until he gave them away to the Salvation Army. He found out when he divided the cost of the shoes by the number of days he wore them that the shoes had cost him nine cents a day. Only a Melancholy would care!

Another man dates every light bulb in his house at the time of purchase. This way he is able to keep a record of each bulb and know the exact length of service.

A girl at CLASS (Christian Leaders and Speakers Seminars) took her Personality Profile and divided it into percentages proving she was 82.5 percent Melancholy. Not that we needed proof!

One father kept a file box on all his son's dates with full family background and his candid opinion of each one. The girl that married him was not pleased when she found her report that said, "Surely, he won't marry this one!" (YPT/46-47)

□   □   □

One Melancholy young man told me he had a date with a Sanguine girl. He went to her office to pick her up on time. He was appalled at the condition of her desk, and also at the fact she had gone on an errand and didn't seem to remember their engagement. As he sat, waiting, he noticed the desk next to hers was meticulous. The desk calendar had neat entries; the pencils were lying

155

with their sharpened points in one direction; and the IN and OUT baskets were empty. The girl with the prize desk came in, and he began to talk with her. She was dressed attractively and seemed to know what she was doing.

"Suddenly," he said, "I could see I was after the wrong girl. The first one never showed up anyway, so I took the second to lunch and we've been dating — in an orderly fashion — ever since." (PPL/49)

□   □   □

In a day and age where mediocrity is accepted as above average, the Melancholy shines as a beacon of high standards for the rest of us to follow. (PPL/50)

□   □   □

The Sanguine is up and down by the minute, and the Melancholy is up and down by the month. (PPL/54)

□   □   □

At one of our marriage seminars, Fred decided to survey what percentage of the Melancholies were musical. He asked a neatly dressed man heading into the Melancholy group to count up how many of the Melancholies were musical. It seemed like a simple request.

Had we asked a Sanguine, she would have gone into her group and said, "How many of you are musical?" (If she remembered to do it at all.) They would all have raised their hands because Sanguines always want to be whatever seems to be popular today, and they all know how to find music on a radio. A Choleric would have made a quick and realistic accounting and proceeded with the other items of business. The Phlegmatic would have asked, but even musical Phlegmatics wouldn't raise their hands for fear the question would lead them into some involvement or require them to join something. So what did the Melancholies do?

When the meticulous man returned, he came forward with his clipboard and a lengthy report. "Fred asked me to see how many people in our group were musical. I asked the question and no one responded. They were thinking. After awhile one said, 'How do you define musical?' That brought a murmur of mutual concern. 'Is musical someone who plays an instrument or someone who appreciates music?' We discussed this for awhile and decided we needed to make two counts: one for those who played instruments and one for those with appreciation for music. I then asked for all those who played to raise their hands. As I counted, a lady asked, 'How about if you used to play the piano when you were a child?' We talked it over and accepted her. Then a man asked, 'What if you're going to start guitar lessons next week?' We let him in and made three counts: Past, present, and future. Next I questioned, 'How many of you appreciate music?' A young lady asked, 'What kind?' We finally divided our question into three sections: Classical, Contemporary, and Gospel. I've added up all the totals in our six-part report and here it is."

He then read his complicated six-part report, and the results showed that all but a few of the Melancholies were musical in some sense and that they were detail-conscious and perfectionists. (GAD/49-50)

157

□   □   □

The *Melancholies* are just the opposite of the Sanguines. They are deep, thoughtful, introspective, philosophical, analytical, artistic, and musical. *However,* they focus on the negatives, are very critical of other people, and get easily depressed. Their *aim* is if it's worth doing, it's worth doing right. Their *compulsion* is to get life, and everyone around them, in perfect order. They usually marry Sanguines to lighten and brighten their lives, but when they get them home, they no longer think they're funny. (GAD/37)

□   □   □

Melancholies who have one-track lives need others who can at least show interest, if not ability, in their field. Musical Melancholies love harmony and balance in life. They are very analytical and deep, and they want to define their terms. (GAD/48)

□   □   □

What do Melancholies want? People who are like them or who show sympathetic interest in their chosen field. If you find their subject of interest they will be glad to converse; if you don't they won't bring it up, but will sit quietly, assuming that no one there is very bright.

What do Melancholies *not* want? Anyone who upsets their systematic way of life or who suggests that they throw caution to the wind and just have a good time. (GAD/50)

□   □   □

The Melancholy's deep analytical thinking is a genius trait, much respected by those of lighter minds; yet, carried to extremes, he becomes brooding and depressed. (PPL/83)

□   □   □

Since the Melancholies are not people-oriented, and have difficulty feeling at ease at social functions, you will be their friend for life if you can rescue them from a lonely corner and ask about their area of expertise. You can be sure they have one, so ask a few leading questions. They tend to give simple answers until you hit their pet topic. (GAD/51)

□   □   □

Once you Melancholies realize what you are doing with your moods, you can begin to improve. As the Sanguine has to force himself to get organized, you have to force yourself to be cheerful. As I explained this principle to my son, he countered, "But I don't *feel* cheerful."

"You don't have to *feel* cheerful, just *be* cheerful. I'd rather have phony *joy* than genuine depression." (PPL/106)

□   □   □

Because of their inborn negative inclinations, Melancholies focus their judgment most harshly upon themselves. They tend to feel insecure in social situa-

159

tions. They are usually attracted to Sanguine mates who can do their conversing for them. I've met brilliant Melancholies, nationally known in their fields, who appeared to be terrified they might be asked to say a few words at a dinner party. The Melancholy's low self-image often comes from criticism given them by their parents and teachers when they were young. Since the Melancholy soaks up negatives, people tend to put more on them. I've noticed in women's club work that presidents who let criticism get to them, get picked on. Those who don't let it bother them are left alone. (PPL/110)

□   □   □

Melancholies have the greatest potential for success. Don't be your own worst enemy. Because the Melancholies are perfectionists, they often refrain from starting certain projects because they are afraid they won't do them right. While the Phlegmatic procrastinates in hopes he won't have to do it, the Melancholy holds back because he has to do it perfectly. (PPL/111)

□   □   □

If Melancholies didn't spend so much time in planning, they wouldn't force the rest of us incompetents to go ahead without preparation and so botch up intricate work! Because the Melancholies place high standards on others, this trait becomes a weakness. (PPL/112)

□   □   □

Although they avoid drawing attention to themselves, the Perfects can become sensitive character actors for they have a unique ability to put themselves into the life of another person and portray their innermost feelings. (PPO/26-27)

❑   ❑   ❑

Once you recognize a Melancholy, you know that you can have a deep and meaningful conversation and that he will appreciate a serious and sincere approach. The Melancholy does not enjoy loud comments, and he will not like it if you draw attention to him. He would rather have one intelligent conversation in an evening than to flit from person to person as the Sanguine does. (PPL/165)

❑   ❑   ❑

The Perfects sensed from childhood that it was better to be right than popular. With an inbred sense of propriety and manners, they became model children who kept their rooms neat, their toys in even rows, and their Monopoly money in the box. They pleased their teachers by raising their hands before speaking, by passing in their papers on time, and by turning in the truants. (PPO/25)

❑   ❑   ❑

Until you understand the Melancholy, you don't realize that they come prepackaged with a pessimistic view of life. This trait is a positive, because they are able to look ahead and see the problems other temperaments don't notice. (PPL/172)

□   □   □

Because the Melancholies are insecure in the love of others, they look with question on the compliments they receive. While the Sanguine is so eager for good words, he will take an insult and turn it into a compliment, the Melancholy often takes a compliment and turns it into an insult! Another reason for their doubt of a casual, uplifting word is they are analytical of everything and suspicious of people, especially happy people. They feel there must be an ulterior motive behind a compliment, and yet they really want to be appreciated. This conflict makes it difficult for anyone to give a positive word to a Melancholy and have it received as it was intended. Knowing this problem should help you to give sincere, quiet, and loving compliments, and not to be upset if the response is "What did you really mean by that?" (PPL/174)

Melancholy/Perfect Parent

The Perfect Parent is what all the others wish they were; clean, neat, organized, punctual, thoughtful, analytical, detail-conscious, compassionate, talented, dedicated, musical, patient, artistic, creative, poetic, sensitive, sincere, and steadfast. Could you ask for anything more? The Perfect Parent takes on the raising of children as a serious life-time project, and indeed it is, but no other personality so totally dedicates itself to producing Perfect children.

Often this parent resists using the four personalities as a tool because it seems too simple, seems to put unfair labels on people, and can't be found spelled out in Scripture. However, once they decide to give it a fair trial (since they are analytical people), they find the simplicity explains complex issues. They learn the labels are needed to break personality down into understandable units, and the theory becomes a useful tool to obey what the Bible commands in examining ourselves, finding our sins, failures, and weaknesses, and bringing them before the Lord for forgiveness and cleansing. (RTC/55-56)

□   □   □

When both parent and child are Perfect Melancholy, everything is done "decently and in order." Rooms are neat, charts are checked, homework is completed on time, research projects are a positive experience. This combination produces child prodigies as each one is dedicated to intellectual pursuits and neither one minds if practice is boring or the routine's dull as long as the goal is a worthy one. What would be too slow for the Powerful Choleric, too dreary for the Popular Sanguine, and too much work for the Peaceful Phlegmatic, is just right for the Perfect. (RTC/56)

□   □   □

The uniting of a Perfect Parent with a Peaceful child will produce a low-key, reticent relationship. The parent will be grateful for the quiet, pleasant, agreeable traits that don't cause any noisy conflicts, but they will be discouraged when this child has no interest in serious dedication to any project in life and will assume that they must be a poor parent because they can't get this child

163

excited over the violin. (RTC/58)

□   □   □

Without a knowledge of the different personalities, [the Perfect Parent and Sanguine child] combination could produce disaster. The Perfect Melancholy Parent expects each child to do things on time and correctly, and can't understand when he discovers this child doesn't have a serious thought or an organized mind. Whatever the parent says, the child has a funny answer and he refuses to get deeply involved in anything. These two tend to bring out the worst in each other. The Perfect Parent gets depressed and feels like a failure when he can't locate this child on a chart. When this Sanguine child gets none of the praise he so desperately needs for survival, he loses any will to perform. His lack of organization and indifferent attitude toward schedules further depresses his parent who becomes critical and nitpicking. These negatives make him feel hopeless, he shuts down his bubbling personality, and saves his humor for people who will appreciate him. (RTC/59)

□   □   □

When I held a seminar in Palm Springs, a very elegant Melancholy lady came up to talk with me. "I've never heard of the temperaments before, and I'm wondering if this could explain what's wrong with my peculiar child."

She then told about the "normal" standards in her home. She, her husband, and one son were Melancholy, and they kept everything just right. She placed the magazines on the coffee table in a perfect row, with each one down far enough to expose the name of the one under it. The magazines were exactly two inches from the edge of the table, and they were always the current issues. No one could read a magazine until the next issue came, so they would always look fresh and crisp.

One day her "peculiar son" (who was ten) walked into the living room, pushed all the magazines off onto the floor, grabbed one, ripped the cover off, crumpled it up, and threw it at her feet. She had been so distraught at this abnormal behavior that she had made an appointment for her son with a child psychiatrist.

As we discussed the problem, I shared with her that while the Melancholy felt having everything perfect was normal, this kind of constant pressure was enough to drive a Sanguine child wild. The boy couldn't take this dollhouse existence any longer. Knowing the temperaments is such a help in dealing with others. The lady had high standards that were great for her and the other two Melancholies, but put upon a Sanguine they were impossible. As she understood this she said, "I thought he was a mental case."

"He will be if you keep this up," I replied. (PPL/112-113)

□ □ □

The Powerful Choleric child wants to do what's right in his or her own sight and if that happens to coordinate with your perfectionistic nature, you two will do well. In contrast to the Popular Sanguine child, the Powerful knows what day of the week it is and can usually out-think his parents automatically. The Powerful has a natural desire for control and your aim is not to shut down his leadership ability but to keep the two of you on the same side. If you hold this aim in mind you will emphasize whenever you agree and tell him constantly how much you appreciate his helping you to run the family. With steady affirmation of the work he is doing, he will become dedicated to high achievement, and he will do half your work for you. He will even remember to check off his chart and do odd jobs you didn't assign him! (RTC/63)

Melancholy-Phlegmatic

[A] natural blend is the Melancholy-Phlegmatic. They are both introverted, pessimistic, and soft-spoken. They are more serious, they look into the depths of situations, and they don't want to be center stage. They follow Teddy Roosevelt's advice, "Speak softly and carry a big stick." The Peaceful Phlegmatic lightens the depth of the Perfect Melancholy, and the Melancholy pulls together the looseness of the Phlegmatic.

This combination makes the greatest educators as the Melancholies' love of study and research is brightened by the Phlegmatics' ability to get along with people and present material in a pleasant manner. They may have trouble in decision making because they both are slow in this area, and they both procrastinate. The best combination is one in which the evenness of the Phlegmatic keeps the Melancholy from dropping into depressions, and the Melancholy's desire for perfection gets the Phlegmatic motivated to action. (PPL/144)

Melancholy-Sanguine

If you come out one-half Popular Sanguine and one-half Perfect Melancholy, our experience shows that one of these two is a mask put on for survival at some point in life. What could have caused this? Usually some type of physical, emotional, sexual or verbal abuse was so severe or so repetitive that the child shut down his or her normal God-given personality and put on a mask to cover up the pain. (FYM/38-39)

□   □   □

Since the Melancholy-Sanguine combination in one person is an unnatural blend, that individual's insides are in a constant war. Their personality is split between Sanguine self-centeredness and Melancholy self-sacrifice. They want to give their all, and yet they need credit for doing it. This combination leads to "a double-minded man, unstable in all his ways." "Like a wave of the sea driven with the wind and tossed" (James 1:8,6). (GAD/85)

□   □   □

In our CLASS counseling we have found that many of the Melancholy-Sanguines were initially Sanguines who went through some very difficult childhood experiences. (GAD/85)

MEN

Fred did a study on God's guide to men and

women, and he found that every time God speaks to both husbands and wives, He addresses the wives first. Do you know why? Men often tell me it's because the women need it more; they're not so bright; it takes them longer to catch on. I have found that women are more aware of their problems and more receptive to spiritual truth. While men are ordained of God to be the spiritual leaders, they have the mistaken idea that to be spiritual is to be a sissy. That concept is not true; it takes a real man to discipline his life and to apply scriptural truth to himself and his family. Becoming a better man is not easy. (AEW/106)

MOTHERS

In this era when women have been told that having children is old-fashioned, it is fascinating to see that even those who follow this trend still have maternal instincts. They don't have the time for a child who needs to be fed, but the researchers for Cabbage Patch found that these women would buy dolls to mother. (OCP/24)

□   □   □

The Cabbage Patch Kid appeals not only to children but to mothers who see their children growing up and not needing them anymore. The maternal instinct, the desire to care for something helpless, is so strong in us women that even if our rational minds tell us we don't want children, we still respond to the outstretched arms of a baby. We all want something that can't get along without us. (OCP/29)

□ □ □

For you young women who are at home with the children, don't let your mind wander out to pasture. Keep alert, keep reading, keep thinking. Know that God will give you a ministry when He feels you are ready. Don't wait until you can see the handwriting on the wall; use every available mental moment to prepare *today* for God's call *tomorrow*. (ITS/15)

N

NEW MORALITY

It does not take a team of researchers to come up with the conclusion that the "new morality" has dropped disaster upon the American family. Some social scientists say it is only a matter of time before the traditional family fades into the sunset. Doomsday proponents compare us with the Roman Empire before its fall and Germany before the rise of Hitler. Wedding ceremonies are often turned to nightmares by the hostile appearance of mother and stepdad seated next to father and stepmother, all of whom hate each other. Should we all give up and run off to Tahiti to find ourselves? Is there anywhere to turn for help? (AEW/68)

O

OBEDIENCE

God doesn't ask a lot of us. He's not unreasonable, but He does expect obedience and honesty.

When God's people follow his clear directions, He blesses them, provides for them, and saves them.

When God's people disobey or are deceptive, He punishes them, teaches them, and forgives them.

What simple truths! What wonderful principles to use in the raising of our own children. (LFG/122)

OUTLINING

God created order and yet so many of our minds are floating in limbo, with thoughts, even inspired thoughts, unattached to any form of organization. Is it not logical that if our minds are fuzzy our daily lives can't be much better? If we wish to be ABOVE AVERAGE, we must train our minds to do what they were originally made for: to think in logical order, to outline life! (ITS/80)

P

PARENTS/PARENTING

God used great wisdom when He told us that we should not live with our in-laws. When we are mature enough to accept the responsibility of marriage, we should leave our father and start a new life. This advice seems so obvious, and yet many couples today have left home physically but are still bound to Mother emotionally.

Martin said, "Mama never approved of my wife. She told me right from the start, 'That girl's not good enough for you—she's trash.' I bucked her for a few years and then she began to point out flaws in Mitzi and I listened. Nothing Mitzi did was as good as Mother did it. One day Mother said, 'Why don't you move back home and let me give you the treatment you deserve?' I left Mitzi for Mama and I'm so ashamed!" (AEW/113)

□   □   □

Why is it we will study, work, and practice on so many pursuits and yet let our family run on its own? We take no basic training and we assume that by nature we will happen to be godly parents. If this miracle happened more than infrequently, we would not have the abundance of family problems we face today. No business, play, or team could win without a leader. No family drama can make it to the last act without a director. God gave parents authority over their children, not so they could exercise tyrannical control, but so they could guide, coach, and instruct their children from their cumulative experience and spiritual wisdom. (RTC/102)

□   □   □

God wants us to have harmony, agreement, and unity, but this bliss does not drop down from heaven; we have to work at it. In the Old Testament newly married couples took a year off to get to know each other and establish unity before they had children. Today many couples get married, both work each day, and they arrive home too exhausted to have meaningful conversations or make long-range, harmonious plans. Many couples have no framework of reference such as the four personality types and some feel that if they're both Christians everything will turn out all right. If that were true we would have no problem Christian marriages or no mixed up Christian teens (and I would have no work!). But since I have people standing in line at every conference desperate for help in their marriages and overwhelmed with their children's problems, I know there is a need. (RTC/103-104)

□   □   □

Without consistency on the part of the parent, no discipline program will work. We could read every child-raising book in the world, but if we didn't follow through on what we said we'd do, the system just wouldn't work. If you mean business with your children, you'll meet to set the basic rules, you'll give clear instructions, you'll observe behavior patterns, you'll ask for written plans for improvement, you'll establish a check-back time and be there, and you'll show the children in a family meeting that good behavior blesses the whole family and that disobedience hurts everyone. (RTC/118)

□   □   □

Our theory was "you may live at home until you get married as long as you go to school or work, and as long as you contribute in some positive way to the household." Lauren lived at home while attending California State University, San Bernardino. She also worked in our restaurant, helped with the housework, and kept reasonable hours as we had agreed. We allowed her to have friends in our home, but it was up to her to see that they adhered to the family rules. Lauren lived with us until she was married at twenty, and we can honestly say that neither she nor her friends ever gave us any trouble. One rule was that everyone in our home came down to breakfast when Fred played the chimes each morning. We were never sure how many would appear. Young people who never got up for breakfast at their own homes (assuming they had it served to them), or warmed up a frosted raspberry Poptart, cheerfully arrived at our table without coaxing.

Marita lived with us until she married at twenty-four. The day she was eighteen she gave Fred and me a personal declaration of independence. She and her friends had discussed that they were now "of age" and no longer had to do anything their parents requested. Coming to breakfast had always been an important family time of togetherness and Marita chose to rebel on that point along with a few others. She would no longer abide by our basic rules unless she "felt like it." Having had such an easy time with Lauren, we were unprepared for this unexpected decree from Marita. For once I didn't know what to say, but I didn't need to, for Fred took charge. Using our agreement principle—when attacked, find something you can agree with as a starter—he acknowledged she did have all these rights that she and her friends had outlined for their parents' approval. She gave a satisfied smile until he added, "but that is only when you live outside of our home. If you wish to live here, you will abide by the rules and be at breakfast in the morning."

This statement was followed by heated questions such as, "Would you pay for me to rent a place?"

"Absolutely not."

Several times I was ready to give in to a few things, but Fred held lovingly firm. By the time Marita went crying to her room, declaring that we didn't understand, I was sure we'd lost her for good. All night I waited for the sound of the squeaky front door hinge. When I didn't hear it, I thought she might have gone out the window. She'd done that before, but when the breakfast chimes sounded in the morning, Marita appeared as bouncy and happy as ever.

We didn't discuss that situation for several years and when we did, she shrugged and said, "It was worth giving it a try." (RTC/111-112)

THE PAST

So many marriages are doomed forever because of past mistakes. The partners are unforgiving and are constantly digging up what happened ten years ago. Whenever a disagreement arises they reach into their bag of tricks and find their two favorite words: always and never. *Always* goes with everything bad and *never* goes with everything good, such as:

"You are *always* late."

"You *never* say a kind word."

The past becomes so much a part of today that there is no hope for the future. Years from now we'll still be trudging down this dreary trail because we've *always* had problems and things will *never* get better. When you look at these thoughts on paper, you can easily see that a constant review of the bad past precludes any improvement in the future. Yet there is hope once we realize the rut we're in and want to rise out of it. Paul says, "The one thing I do . . . is to forget what is behind me and do my best to reach what is ahead" (Philippians 3:13, TEV). (AEW/93-94)

□   □   □

What should you do if someone does open up and disclose some past hurts? Sometimes seeing the connection between the past and present will be healing in itself.

1. Let the person talk it out, as a compassionate listener can be a physician to the soul.

2. Refer the individual to a Christian counselor who deals with past pain and won't just tell the person to forget it.

3. Help him or her find a person trained in emotional inner healing using Christian principles.

4. In extreme cases, find a psychologist who can lead him or her through some regressive therapy. (GAD/88)

PERSPECTIVE

Often after I have listened to the terrible description of an obvious ogre of a husband I ask the angry woman, "How did an intelligent lady like you ever get attracted to such a loser? What did you see in him in the first place?"

Usually her response is, "Well, he used to be different. When I first met him he was handsome, witty, generous . . ."

"What caused all this to change?"

"Not everything changed. He's actually still good-looking if he'd ever smile. He can be funny at parties, though he's dull as dishwater at home. He's still generous with the kids, but he wouldn't give me a nickel."

It's always easy for an outsider to see that there are still good points in this man, but she seems to bring out the worst in him. Is he really such a rat? What is there positive about this person? (AEW/93)

PHLEGMATICS/PEACEFULS

The Phlegmatic tones down the wild schemes of the Sanguine.

The Phlegmatic refuses to get too impressed with the brilliant decisions of the Choleric.

The Phlegmatic doesn't take too seriously the intricate plans of the Melancholy.

The Phlegmatic is the great leveler of us all, showing us, "It doesn't really matter that much." And in the long run, it really doesn't! We are all part of a complex plan in which each temperament, when functioning properly, will fit into the right place and unite to form an exciting and balanced picture. (PPL/69)

□   □   □

The Peaceful babies were every mother's dream. They seldom cried, slept through the night, and didn't care if they were wet or dry. As toddlers they smiled pleasantly, played with anything available, and loved naps. When the Popular children came over, the Peacefuls laughed at all their antics. They could get serious and deep with the Perfects and were motivated into action by the Powerfuls. They were responders to the initiators of life.

As teens they got along with everyone. They would laugh with those who laughed and weep with those who wept. They never demanded their own way and were never offensive. (PPO/29)

□   □   □

When the Melancholy says I have to think about it, he really thinks about it, but the Phlegmatic uses this expression to postpone action. It isn't that he wants to think; it's that he doesn't want to act. One lady who was taking me out to dinner asked her Phlegmatic husband for his decision on where to go. "Are we still thinking about it or are we ready to do it?"

Making decisions is difficult for the Phlegmatic. I loved the paperweight on a Phlegmatic's desk that carries the message, "Maybe—and that's final." A greeting card showed a Phlegmatic tiger draped over an easy-chair. On the inside it said, "Get up before they make a rug out of you."

Because the Phlegmatics desire peace, they are easy to manipulate and frequently find themselves pushed around by Cholerics who need someone to control. Although they usually will take whatever's handed out, once in a while, to keep peace with themselves, they will refuse to conform and they will hold their ground.(YPT/48-49)

□　　□　　□

I had one Phlegmatic friend who was a great mother to her brood, but housework was not a high priority. If I dropped by in the middle of the morning, the kitchen table would still have the cereal bowls, the open boxes, and the milk from breakfast. We'd both sit down, push the debris to one side, make room for our elbows, and enjoy each other's company. Since the mess didn't bother her, it didn't bother me. (PPL/78-79)

□　　□　　□

The Phlegmatic is the closest there is to being a perfect person: one who does not function in the extremes or excesses of life, but walks solidly down the middle road, avoiding conflict and decision on either side. The perfect person does not offend, does not call atten-

179

tion to himself, and quietly does what is expected of him without looking for credit. While the Choleric is the "born leader," the Phlegmatic is the "learned leader," and with proper motivation can rise to the top because of his outstanding ability to get along with everyone. While the Choleric wants to run everything, the Phlegmatic tends to hold back until asked and is never pushy. (PPL/69-70)

□　□　□

I asked a young boy about his Phlegmatic girlfriend. "What do you like best about her?"

He thought for a minute and said, "I guess all of her, because nothing much stands out." This simple statement sums up the Phlegmatics; there's nothing that really stands out, but they are such comfortable, well-rounded people to be with. They never appear to be conceited and they keep a low profile. One Phlegmatic man said, "I guess I'm just an average person." And another sighed in disbelief, "I'm just amazed when people like me." The humility and gentleness of the Phlegmatic is so pleasing to be with and gives the other temperaments some positive qualities to work on as we all aim for sainthood. (PPL/72)

□　□　□

The Phlegmatic doesn't expect sunshine every day, so when rain falls on his parade he can keep on marching. How much we all could learn from the attitude that accepts life as it is, and is reconciled to reality. (PPL/74-75)

☐   ☐   ☐

Churches have special halos for Phlegmatics. Chatty Sanguines love them because they listen. Controlling Cholerics surround themselves with them because they'll agree to anything. Moody Melancholies appreciate how they adjust to whatever mood you're in today. Phlegmatics are popular in the parish, so what kind of problems could you possibly have with such perfect people?

They tend to avoid responsibility, lack enthusiasm for new projects, and criticize those who take action. They don't feel these are really weaknesses but good judgment. They know better than to assume responsibility for something they shouldn't be doing. Some projects aren't worthy of enthusiasm, and some people are too pushy.

Even though these low-key people dampen others' initiative they do bring balance to aggressive groups and families. The Phlegmatic is the great leveler of life. (GAD/62)

☐   ☐   ☐

In growing up, Phlegmatics find that being average is good enough, but often because they are so amiable they are thrust into positions of leadership. (GAD/63)

☐   ☐   ☐

The Phlegmatic's easygoing nature is an admirable combination that makes him the favorite of any

181

group; yet carried to extremes, the Phlegmatic doesn't care about doing anything and is indifferent and indecisive. (PPL/83)

□   □   □

Phlegmatics provide a placid plateau without problems. Once you accept that they won't get excited and will flee from controversy, you'll have no troubles in getting along. If you are courageous, you may try to challenge and motivate them to action, but frequently they'll feel that it's just too much like work. (GAD/65)

□   □   □

One day as I was shopping for Phlegmatic chairs—ones that are quiet and unobtrusive and will blend with any decor—the thought came to me, *The Phlegmatic's greatest strength is his lack of obvious weaknesses.* The Phlegmatic doesn't have temper tantrums, sink into depressions, or spin his wheels noisily. He just stays unenthusiastic, worries quietly, and can't make decisions. Hardly faults obvious enough to demand correction. (PPL/129)

□   □   □

Phlegmatics: Get enthused. Start with once a month and work up from there. (PPL/131)

□   □   □

The problem of procrastination is prevalent with

both Melancholies and Phlegmatics, but for different reasons. The Melancholy cannot start anything until he has the right equipment and feels he can do a perfect job; but the Phlegmatic postpones because underneath he doesn't want to do it. He tends to be lazy and postponements keep him from making a decision to get to work. The Phlegmatic has a mañana complex: Never do today what you can put off until tomorrow. (PPL/133)

□ □ □

Sharon's mind was like a game of pool. The colorful balls only rolled around when pushed, and had for years clustered cozily in a mesh bag, hanging securely in the corner.

It wasn't that she couldn't move; it was just too much like work. When properly motivated, she could pull a few balls out of the pocket and roll them around the fertile green, as long as the occasion demanded. When the pressure relaxed, she would clear the table and retreat to her net, until someone in exasperation would grab the colored balls, throw them across the green and cry, *"Move!"*

This simple little parable is typical of the Phlegmatic. It's not that they *can't* do the job; it's that they don't *want* to. One lady told me she had cut out at least four dresses, but it was just too much like work to sew them up. "If I ever need one for a special occasion, I'll do it." (PPL/134)

□ □ □

You Phlegmatics deserve to be henpecked if you

can't motivate yourselves to responsible action (PPL/134)

□   □   □

By keeping his mouth shut the Phlegmatic stays out of trouble much of the time, but by hiding his feelings and refusing to communicate, he stifles any meaningful relationship with others. (PPL/136)

□   □   □

The Phlegmatic's problem with making decisions is not that he is incompetent, but that he has made one great decision never to make any decisions. After all, if you don't make the decision, you're not held accountable for the outcome. (PPL/136)

□   □   □

Phlegmatics: Learn to say no and practice making decisions. Start with chocolate and vanilla, if all thirty-one flavors are just too much to cope with at once! (PPL/137)

□   □   □

Phlegmatics tend to band together at parties and sit quietly. There is a certain comfort in knowing that they don't expect anything of each other, and that they can mutually bask in each other's acceptance of the status quo. If you are looking for an audience or for someone who won't argue with you, try a Phlegmatic. You'll like him. (PPL/166)

Phlegmatic/Peaceful Parent

The Peaceful Parent has the kind, low-key, relaxed, patient, sympathetic nature that we find so agreeable and acceptable in a father or mother. They don't argue or fight, they don't insist on high achievement, they roll with the punches, and they're never irrational or hysterical. What more could any child want? (RTC/64)

□   □   □

The Peaceful [Parent]/Peaceful [child] combination is ideal in that both parent and child agree that life is "no big deal." There's nothing to get excited over. Let's not "sweat the small stuff."

One couple told me their baby was born so Phlegmatic that for the first month they thought she was in a coma. She didn't care whether she ate or not, and they sometimes woke her up to make sure she was still alive! Amazingly we can often tell the personality of a baby very early when we know what we're looking for.

The little Peaceful child is the easiest to raise, especially for a Peaceful Parent. My son-in-law Randy and his father are both Peacefuls. His father told me how as a child Randy was so adaptable that wherever they took him he would sit quietly and read. He would sleep anywhere and eat at any time. The problem with this pair of Peacefuls comes later in life when the child is not motivated and the parent doesn't care, or the child wants to get into some sport and the parent feels it's just too much like work. One other weakness in these parents is their ability to overlook the truth if it will save them work. The Peaceful person often finds a little white lie a useful, if not admirable, tool. (RTC/64-65)

□　　□　　□

On Easter Sunday as the family was gathered, I asked my Peaceful son-in-law Randy, "Can you think of any example of you as a Peaceful father with Bryan, a Powerful son?" He thought and said, "No I can't." At that point, two-year-old Bryan sat down on the grass next to Marita's two Schnauzer puppies and their dish of food. As Bryan began to feed them, I noticed he was putting one piece of kibble into each puppy's mouth and then one into his own little mouth. I pointed out to Randy, "Your son is eating dog food."

"Don't do that, Bryan. Don't eat the dog's food, little Bryan," Randy said softly.

Bryan looked him straight in the eye, picked up one more piece, stuck it in his mouth, and smiled at his father.

Typically Randy shrugged and replied, "Oh well, a little dog food won't kill him." I laughed and we both realized what a perfect example he'd given me of the Peaceful father who made token resistance to the strong child and when he found out that to implement his direction he'd have to get up and walk across the lawn, it wasn't worth the effort.

It is always easier for the Peaceful Parent not to buck the Powerful child, but this Choleric is a smart, aggressive child. If he can control at two, watch out when he hits thirteen! The Peaceful Parents are always the best loved because they are easy-going, pleasant to get along with, and they don't really care what the child is doing. (RTC/66)

□   □   □

The similarities in the Peaceful Parent and the Perfect child are that they are both natural introverts, they tend to be pessimistic, they don't initiate conversations, and they need to be inspired to get down to work. When you bestow upon the Peaceful Parent a Perfect child, the combination can be quiet and respectful because of their similarities, but when the quiet child withdraws and becomes depressed, the Peaceful Parent prefers not to deal with the problem. It's easier to avoid it and hope it goes away. (RTC/68)

□   □   □

In contrast to the Perfect child, the Popular child usually brings out the humorous side of the Peaceful Parent who loves to have a good time as long as someone else is preparing the party. The Popular child loves to instigate parties as long as someone will come. The Populars are all a constant source of entertainment and they thrive on response. The Peacefuls are responders to the circumstances around them so they provide a perfect balance. Once the Peacefuls get involved in a humorous repartee, their dry wit often produces the funniest lines and they become downright Sanguine.

Because they are responders and not initiators, the Peacefuls react to the people they are with more than any other type does. They become whatever it's right to be today. The Peacefuls truly fit the verse, Romans 12:15: "Rejoice with them that do rejoice, and weep with them that weep." (RTC/69)

POLITICAL PERSONALITIES

Barbara Bush

Barbara is a Powerful Personality balancing and completing George's Peaceful nature. She is open, candid, and expressive and isn't worried about what people think of her. She has been the disciplinarian of the family and the caretaker of the home, while her husband has been traveling and working long hours. Before moving into the White House they had lived in twenty-eight houses in seventeen cities and it was Barbara who found each new home and moved into it.

Barbara has the strengths of the Powerful Personality without the abrasiveness that often accompanies these characteristics. (PPO/194)

□   □   □

Many of us women will be glad to have a First Lady who is a size 14 and doesn't look like a Dresden doll. Perhaps the '88 to '92 years will be the era of the average woman. Perhaps we can stop starving ourselves and be proud of the natural look God gave us. (PPO/194)

George Bush

While other candidates had to scrounge for credentials and exaggerate their abilities, George was quietly living an exemplary life. As a Peaceful person, he has been willing, from childhood, to put the other person first and not insist on his own way. He has been generous, well-mannered and gracious. As a child, he was

188

nicknamed by his mother "Have Half" because whenever she gave him a cookie, he would turn to the person beside him and say "have half." (PPO/188)

□ □ □

In all of George Bush's diverse areas of public service, he was considered as a kind, encouraging, soothing, understanding, amiable, witty person, who listened politely to all opinions, tried to take the middle-road, and didn't need to get the credit.

All of these Peaceful strengths are quiet low-key attributes that don't make headlines. When Bush took over the CIA, the agency was trying to recover from exposés and excesses. His "don't-rock-the-boat" attitude calmed the troubled waters and steadied the reeling spyship. He testified in Congress without drawing attention to himself and he quietly healed the hurts of the agency. (PPO/191)

□ □ □

Only the Peaceful Phlegmatic is naturally able to play the role of the bridesmaid when he wanted to be the bride; only the Peaceful can sit in meeting after meeting and not need to make a comment; only a Peaceful can support other people's ideas continually without insisting they adopt a few of his. (PPO/192)

□ □ □

George is everyone's Mr. Nice Guy, every woman's first husband. He brought to the '88 campaign the most impressive credentials in a field of generally un-exciting candidates. He is relaxed, at peace with himself, and naturally polite and gracious. It is often noted that on the day after his three-year-old daughter's death from leukemia, George Bush returned to the hospital and personally thanked each nurse and doctor who had cared for her. He is known for handwriting personal notes to friends and underlings to congratulate, console, or encourage.

Bush is a qualified political servant who modestly refuses to blow his own horn, a decent man who hasn't made major mistakes and who, under press scrutiny, has opened a closet holding no skeletons. (PPO/192)

□   □   □

George Bush is the political model of a Peaceful leader. He is able to mediate between contentious people and moderate hot tempers while staying calmly above the fray. (PPO/196)

□   □   □

In the major positions Bush has held he has come in at a time of trouble, calmed everyone down, brought harmony out of chaos, made differing opinions into unity, and built an effective team, all without drawing attention to himself. These may not be flashy traits, but they could well be what we need in the post-Reagan era. (PPO/196)

□   □   □

George Bush has been known for his ability to

skirt conflict and for his stabilizing influence. He has been and will be a Peaceful leader and, like Gerald Ford, he arrived at the White House with few enemies. His affable nature, expressing no extremes of opinion, adjusts according to each situation and keeps him from offending anyone. (PPO/196)

□   □   □

During the 1988 campaign Bush became a master of his personality strengths and even the Democrats were not able to find anything of significance wrong with him. Bush didn't try to be something he wasn't but kept his middle-of-the-road, easy-going, pleasant personality before the public who finally accepted him as an honest person, a decent moral man, who might not ever be exciting but who would wear well. Even though his managers tried to turn him into a Powerful to enhance his leadership image, he held true to his nature and came through as sincere and genuine. (PPO/197)

□   □   □

Once George Bush had been overwhelmingly elected, winning 40 states with 426 electoral votes to Dukakis' 10 states with 112 electoral votes, the press began to view him through new eyes. They used descriptive words typical of the Peaceful Personality: Extending the peacepipe, minimizing problems, bi-partisan person, reaches out to all, heals wounds, slow-starter, too neutral, lacking depth, obstinate, opaque and elusive. (PPO/197-198)

□   □   □

After years of being number two and winning the election because he tried harder, George Bush became number one, was put in the driver's seat and headed over bumpy roads in hopes of consolidating the electorate and making the United States "a kinder and gentler nation." (PPO/198)

James Earl Carter

James Earl Carter came into office somewhat like a schoolteacher bringing the class back to order after recess. As a nation we'd been somewhat out to lunch, and it was time to get organized again. We'd dealt with the crises during the Kennedy administration, the Vietnam escalation with Johnson, and the Watergate scandal with Nixon. We'd needed a rest time with Ford to regroup our thoughts, and now we were after a restoration of order and ethics. His personality fit the Perfect Melancholy profile right from the beginning as he was an excellent student, loved to read, and was fascinated by engineering. (PPO/102)

□   □   □

Carter knew his potential was in the Perfect assimilation of details. He constantly studied the issues so he would know every possible fact, and he consulted experts on each current topic.

Perfect Jimmy made perfect plans, kept perfect files, and won. (PPO/104)

☐   ☐   ☐

Jimmy scheduled every day ahead, including time for a bathroom break, and he usually kept to within five minutes of his detailed plan. In 1972 he began working on his organizational charts for his presidential bid in 1976. While few knew what he was planning, he had it all mapped out. (PPO/105)

☐   ☐   ☐

Once "Jimmy who?" had won the election in 1976, he began to study all the inaugural addresses of the past presidents in order that he might compose his from a wealth of background. He had no pretensions of grandeur, and he wanted his message to be simple and his demeanor to be humble. He wanted to be a leader on the level with the people, not a lofty king above the crowds. To demonstrate his servant's attitude, he chose to walk in the inaugural parade instead of ride in an open limousine as was the usual custom. (PPO/105)

☐   ☐   ☐

Carter's strong beliefs and his open willingness to talk about God made him different from the passively religious presidents before him, some of whom would well have blushed if asked to give the blessing at a banquet.

Carter came into the Oval Office on his morality, his firm confidence, his amazing self-discipline, his studied knowledge of major issues, his refusal to compromise his standards, and his appeal as an honest outsider. (PPO/106)

193

□　□　□

Carter's confidence gradually eroded as he found that not everyone had his Perfect principles or wished to follow his sincere directions. Inflation wouldn't listen to him, recession continued even when he said stop, and the fuel shortage got worse and worse in spite of his threats. (PPO/106-107)

□　□　□

Carter put so much effort into plotting out his schedules that soon critics said he had become a manager instead of a leader. He had to give up some of his noble, idealistic visions so typical of the Perfect personality, and these losses of great plans began to depress him. (PPO/107)

□　□　□

By his third year in power, Perfect Carter's strengths had turned into weaknesses, and the press began to use words like: aimless, drifting, remote, losing touch, depressed, dismal, frightening. Carter created a memorable phrase when he told us with the heavy heart of the Perfect nature that we were in a "national malaise." What a melancholy word, malaise! The dictionary says malaise is "an indefinite feeling of bodily uneasiness or discomfort." As Jimmy lost his comfort, we all became uneasy. (PPO/107)

□　□　□

Although Jimmy's sincere humility was shown in his walking to the Inaugural and not wearing a tall silk hat, this just-one-of-the-guys attitude was interpreted to denote a lack of strong leadership skills. I'm sure Jimmy meant well, but he misread the public's concept of what constitutes a leader.

Humorous articles on the meaning of leadership were published, and somehow humility wasn't one of the characteristics mentioned. The press ridiculed Jimmy and they seemed to select pictures of him where he looked depressed. Here we had an honest man who sincerely thought that he could straighten out the problems of the country. He'd done his best, he'd run the race, but he didn't win the prize on his second try. (PPO/109)

Dwight David Eisenhower

Ike was typical of the Peacefuls who quietly do what is expected of them, walk the middle line of life and manage to offend no one. They smile, nod in agreement, and pacify the contentious. They will agree with either side of an issue if it will keep people happy. Their low-key personality doesn't mean they have nothing intelligent to say; they just reserve their wit for the right time and have no need to add a comment to every conversation. (PPO/53)

□　　□　　□

In typical Peaceful fashion, he had always quietly done the right thing at the right time, pleased his superiors, and not caused any shock waves anywhere along the line. He had a sense of how to get along with others, and he didn't need to have his own way. His easy-going na-

195

ture, wide grin, and willingness to compromise made him a hit with the hotheads . . . Eisenhower was considered the peace-loving man of war. (PPO/54)

□   □   □

While we all liked Ike, he was never known for exciting or creative ideas or for many innovative programs. But then we asked little of him but that he leave us alone and let us return to normal.

Eisenhower was an all-purpose, middle-of-the-road president whose greatest strength was his lack of obvious weaknesses. (PPO/55)

□   □   □

Critics murmured that Ike was a remote and detached manager who didn't have any idea what was really going on. (PPO/56)

□   □   □

After years of the ultimate Commander-in-Chief, Franklin Roosevelt, who easily controlled with confidence, and the feisty Harry Truman, who "gave 'em hell," the Peaceful, humble, relaxed and smiling Ike was a welcome and restful change. He became president not because of life-long political ambitions, but as the quiet answer to the call of duty. (PPO/57)

□   □   □

He wanted to use his strategic skills to calm the times of tempest, not to fight eternal wars. He was willing to give a little here and there to avoid upsetting anyone, and he didn't need the credit to build up his own ego, a rare trait in a political hero. (PPO/58)

□　□　□

Ike always did what he felt was right, whether or not it was popular. As the old soldier he marched straight ahead, played according to the rules, and always responded to the call of duty. (PPO/59)

Gerald Ford

There was Gerald Ford with his Peaceful personality. Not since the election of Dwight Eisenhower at the end of the war had we been looking for a man of Peace who would take us in his arms and rock us to sleep. When Ford was inaugurated as the 38th president, he even had the Bible open to an appropriate verse from Ecclesiastes: "There is a time to love and a time to hate; a time of war and a time of peace." He told us our "long national nightmare" was over, and he was ready to give us "conciliation, compromise, and cooperation," all words that express the virtues of the Peaceful personality. (PPO/95)

□　□　□

Gerald Ford came in on his strengths: quiet, low-key nature, non-controversial, well-liked by all, calm, cool and collected, totally inoffensive. He came in as the All-Purpose President, a Man for All Seasons, a team player.

He didn't have the impulsive nature of Kennedy, keeping us on the edge of our seats with a combination of fear and excitement. He didn't have the compulsive nature of Nixon, desperately needing to know and tape every thought. He didn't have an ego that cried to be stroked like Johnson. He was just happily surprised to be president after all those years of steady performance in the House of Representatives.

Gerald Ford was almost too good to be true. He surely strolled in on his strengths. (PPO/96)

□   □   □

Ford was a team player whether in football or in politics. He never tried to be the star or do flashy footwork; he just wanted to do his best and be well liked.

Truman, Johnson and Ford all were instant presidents. Like instant rice, they were all dropped into a pot of boiling water and had to expand to fill their roles. (PPO/97)

□   □   □

Ford was nick-named "Mr. Clean" and "Goody-Two-Shoes" because no one knew of anything he'd done wrong. His ability to mediate opposing forces and to smooth down any ruffled feathers was an asset as he headed into the most crucial political position in the country. (PPO/97)

□   □   □

When it was time for Ford to run on his own for reelection, the public accepted the prospect that he would be voted in. He had done nothing wrong although little that could be considered inspirational. He had been inoffensive and had no enemies, however he'd never succeeded in getting us to march to his drum-beat, mainly because he wasn't beating any drums. (PPO/99)

□　□　□

Gerald Ford came in on his Peaceful strengths and left after 895 days on his weaknesses. He just never got out of the chair and ran. He took his defeat calmly, gave no negative condemnations to any of his staff, blamed no one but himself, graciously turned his position of power over to his successor, packed his bags and retired to Rancho Mirage, near Palm Springs. (PPO/99)

Horatio Hubert Humphrey

Horatio Hubert Humphrey was a true Popular and whatever came in his ears went out his mouth without staying around long enough to ferment. He always looked wide-eyed and innocent, and he had a quick answer for every question — not necessarily based on fact. Before LBJ would accept Humphrey, Humphrey had to pledge absolute loyalty and agree never to disagree. He was to try to keep his mouth shut, never upstage Lyndon, and avoid making headlines. (PPO/80)

Lady Bird Johnson

Lady Bird came from a well-feathered nest, and she became a Perfect counter-balance for LBJ's volatile

Powerful personality. Lady Bird was genuinely gracious in a more homespun way than Jackie's regal style of entertaining. For years at the ranch Lady Bird had been hospitable to any number of people at any time, with or without advance notice, for when Lyndon said, "Y'all come," he really meant "you all."

As LBJ was flamboyant, Lady Bird was disciplined and controlled, organized and efficient. As he was Popular, she was willing to give him center stage. As he needed to monologue a message and be the life of the party, she was willing to listen attentively and act as if she'd never heard that line before. As he was prone to exaggeration and had a habitual disregard for the truth, she did her homework, knew her facts, and talked intelligently. (PPO/77)

Lyndon Baines Johnson

There was never any doubt that Lyndon Johnson wanted to be president, but he had not expected to receive the title in such a tragic way. A young Popular-Powerful president had been assassinated, and Lyndon was called to fill his shoes. He had been preparing for this role for years, he'd done his homework, he was ready. He'd been an effective Senate majority leader and he was confident that when he got in control of any situation he could make things happen. He always had. (PPO/76)

□   □   □

LBJ was his own Horatio Alger story. From the time he was a child he wanted to be in charge, and he was constantly convincing others that his way was the right way. He could see early on that politics was the step-ladder to Power, and he wanted to spend as little time as possible on each rung. (PPO/77)

□ □ □

He was a born politician who knew how to twist arms quietly and give people "the Johnson treatment."

"You are a very important person to me and I need your help now." He was a born power-broker; he knew how to use his personal contacts for gain and when to call in his markers. He had used this skill with uncanny results in the Senate, but he soon learned that he had a different cast in the White House. He was a born storyteller, had a legendary charm and wit, and was exhilarated into brilliance by adoring crowds. He would give a lecture on anything, to anyone, at any place, at the drop of a ten-gallon hat. (PPO/78)

□ □ □

Popular people have a desperate need to be loved by all, and they can't bear to think there's anyone who doesn't like them. Powerful people try to stay in control strongly enough that no one will dare turn against them. Johnson, being a bountiful blend of the two, resented any negative comments. He would become like a little hurt boy when the press took him on, and he'd say sadly, "I'm the only president they've got." (PPO/78)

□ □ □

His Powerful nature recoiled at anything he couldn't control, and his Popular personality was infuriated by any kind of criticism. He wanted obedience and adoration, and he was getting neither.

LBJ believed anything is possible if you just work hard enough. When he couldn't end the Vietnam War, his life-long "work ethic" fell apart. He was so proud of the Great Society he was creating out of the fragments of the New Frontier, and he couldn't believe his people wouldn't accept his strengths and overlook his weaknesses. (PPO/81)

□   □   □

Because of his underlying insecurity, he forced himself to be more than charming, more than dynamic, more than successful. He became somewhat of an exaggeration of himself. FDR and JFK each functioned about 50 percent Popular and 50 percent Powerful, but LBJ came across as 100 percent of each. His overwhelming personality made him a 200 percent man. There was a lot of Lyndon! (PPO/82)

Jacqueline Kennedy

Not only did we have a Popular-Powerful president, but we had a Perfect princess. Following Eleanor, Bess and Mamie, hardly a beauty pageant line-up, we had elegant, charming, classy Jackie. We watched everything she wore with covetous attention, and we all ran out to buy pill-box hats.

Jackie had an air of mystery about her as every fairy princess must have, and she seemed so secure in social situations. (PPO/65)

❑   ❑   ❑

Jackie dressed perfectly, charmed dignitaries perfectly, decorated perfectly and entertained perfectly. Jackie was Perfect, and we could understand why she didn't want to play football with the family. No one thought of asking how much she spent on clothes or whether she borrowed her gowns from French designers. (PPO/66)

John F. Kennedy

With the close victory of Kennedy over Nixon, we were transported into Fairyland. Pack up the Depression and the Wars in an old kit bag and smile, smile, smile. Jack always smiled. (PPO/65)

❑   ❑   ❑

Jack's presenting personality was Popular. He was fun-loving, charming, even intoxicating. He exuded sex-appeal, whether in a T-shirt or in a tuxedo. He had a sense of humor, was a spontaneous storyteller, and was always the center of attention. He was able to look presidential without being pompous, and could shine brightly while standing next to superstars. (PPO/66)

❑   ❑   ❑

Jack's Powerful nature made him a fast mover, and a highly competitive opponent. When he walked into a room he had instant control, and he used his ability to manipulate skillfully and without effort. His father had put an emphasis on ability and the pursuit of excellence, and he endorsed these principles wholeheartedly. (PPO/70)

□   □   □

His quest for the best caused him to be impatient with those not meeting his standards, to be irritated by those who didn't move quickly, and to be annoyed by the "dummies of life" with whom he occasionally had to deal. His desire for action covered a fear of boredom, and he was uncomfortable whenever he was not in control. (PPO/70)

□   □   □

When we look at the Popular part of Kennedy's personality we see the inborn traits of making life fun, looking through rose-colored glasses, desiring the adulations of the crowd, and wanting everyone to love him. With these strengths came his overemphasis on illusions vs. reality and his deceptive way of making us think he was accomplishing more than was actually going on. Indeed, many political pundits recognize that Kennedy's popularity was rooted more in fiction than reality.

His Powerful side gave him the innate drive for success so easily harnessed by both his father and mother, the need to be a winner and not a runner-up, and the obsession with masculine strength and control. When we add these personality patterns together and stuff them into a handsome man with an abundance of charisma, we can see what a product old Joe had that he could package and sell to the American public. (PPO/71)

□   □   □

As a country we let him pull us to happy-ever-after-land, because we wanted to believe. When we found he didn't know the way and hadn't counted the cost, we were surprised. We didn't realize he had no serious destination in mind and that he agreed with the ad, "getting there is half the fun," but we were willing to overlook his mistakes because he'd given us a vicarious vision of royalty, and we wanted to live happily ever after in a castle.

Suddenly it was over, our hero was gone, reality hit hard. We all cried as we watched John-John at the funeral; we admired Jackie's presence and composure; we said good-bye to our version of a king. (PPO/74)

Richard Nixon

Young Richard learned early in life that he was not popular or particularly handsome, so he opted to develop his mind. He became obsessed with the mastery of details and needed to know everything about every subject. He found that perfect knowledge is power and when you have perfect control of facts you can soon control people and situations and have power.

He stayed remote and emotionally uninvolved with people, and was nicknamed, "Gloomy Gus." (PPO/87)

□   □   □

Because Nixon saw himself as being left out on the lawn alone, he wanted desperately to win the presidential plum on his own. As a Perfect-Powerful, he was going to do it right and show them he didn't need to ride on anyone's coattails. (PPO/64)

□   □   □

Nixon has been a clear example of the principle that a strength carried to extreme becomes a weakness. The strengths of his anxieties led him to study deeply, memorize facts, train his brilliant mind, win debates and get a scholarship to law school. The weaknesses manifested later caused him to have a compulsive need to win, even if he had to bend the rules to do so. (PPO/88-89)

□   □   □

Without Watergate Nixon would have ranked as one of our most brilliant and successful presidents. He will still be remembered as something of a Shakespearean heroe, a great man with a tragic flaw. His childhood insecurities and inferiorities taught him that knowledge was power and that he needed all he could get. Experience showed him that even with a mastery of the details he could still lose and so he took no chances.

His childhood fear of people knowing his inner thoughts . . . grew into a fetish in his presidential years. He was so afraid someone would tap his wires while he was taping their words. (PPO/91-92)

□   □   □

Richard Nixon still has unprecedented comprehension of government intricacies and foreign policy, but now his vast knowledge can produce only limited power. He is a brilliant man, a tragic hero with a near-fatal flaw.

Richard Nixon came in on his strengths and left on his weaknesses. (PPO/93)

Dan Quayle

On the afternoon of August 16, 1988, as George Bush alighted from the riverboat Natchez, he stood before cheering crowds on the Spanish Plaza under impending thunderclouds, and announced his choice for the Republican vice-presidential nominee. The decision had not been anticipated until later in the convention and the Bush announcement took the people by surprise. Many had no idea what George had said or who Quayle was. Murmurs grew to shouts, "What did he say?" "Dan who?" "Who's a quail?" "Let's see him."

Suddenly a handsome young man smiling in wild disbelief emerged from the crowds and bounded toward the vice-president. He whipped off his jacket and joked, "Actually, I was just in the area and stopped by."

With his boyish charm and Robert Redford looks, Danny brought out maternal instincts in many of us and gasps of admiration in others. When he turned to give George Bush an appreciative hug, he almost knocked him over with enthusiasm and eagerness to get on with the campaign.

As with every personality, each one comes equipped with both strengths and weaknesses. The media did instant studies on Dan Quayle and found him to have the engaging Popular attributes: He was sunny, affable, talkative, humorous, charming, magnetic, eager to please, exuberant, rambunctious, energetic, engaging, naive, trusting, ingenious, wholesome, loveable, and sparkling.

Within twenty-four hours of his selection, Dan Quayle displayed some of the Popular weaknesses. At times when he opened his mouth he seemed to put his foot in it. When faced by a probing and aggressive media he looked confused and upset. (PPO/201-202)

◻   ◻   ◻

Quayle's favorite movie is *The Candidate* starring his look-alike Robert Redford. His life parallels the plot line of the show but handsome Dan Quayle is no longer a candidate; he's the Vice President of the United States.

Time is on Quayle's side now and, as Populars often do, he will probably turn his negatives into positives. (PPO/203)

Nancy Reagan

Even though the press has fussed about the First Lady borrowing her wardrobe from Galanos and Adolfo, I personally think a lending library of designer fashions is a brilliant idea. (PPO/155)

Ronald Reagan

Ronald Reagan appeared on the national stage on call. We had been viewing the *Tragedy of Watergate* with the Shakespearean hero, King Richard, a brilliant brooding man with a tragic flaw, and we had been placated by the plotless pantomime at the Ford Theatre. We had become depressed over the deep drama of Mr. Everyman, carrying his own suitcase and retreating to Camp David and we were sick of those bags of peanuts at intermission. We were ready for a star who knew he could lead us and had been trained for it. We wanted a Popular President to take charge and let us smile again. (PPO/121)

□   □   □

Not only did the plot progress, according to Reagan's plan, but he and Nancy wore their costumes well and moved Hollywood glitter and glamour to the grey stages of Washington. They placed themselves against a variety of sparkling backdrops, kept fireworks blazing, flags waving, and balloons bursting forth. They marched to colorfully costumed bands, cried to the tune of funeral dirges, and waltzed to Lester Lanin and his society orchestra. (PPO/122)

□   □   □

Our Popular President was not only the All-American boy of "amiable averageness" floating above the mundane problems of life, but he was also a magician. The term, "the Reagan magic," had been used from the beginning to mean two things. One, he had such charisma that he drew people to him like a magnet and, two, he could get involved in sticky situations, face adverse circumstances that would have overwhelmed Ford and put Carter on valium, wave his magic wand and come out smelling like the proverbial rose. (PPO/124)

□   □   □

Reagan used his humor to entertain, to defuse tension, and to help himself relax. Once he had the first laughing response in a speech, he was at ease. He would often stray from the text to insert a story. Speaking on the shores of Lake Michigan, he ad libbed, "Being here along the lake reminds me of a story—when you're my age, everything reminds you of a story." (PPO/127)

□   □   □

Along with Reagan's sense of humor came his unique ability to personalize politics. He could take a complex issue and bring it into focus by making a personal analogy that the public can understand. (PPO/128)

□   □   □

Much to the dismay of his opponents, Reagan can hold an audience better than anyone else. His years of acting experience, his natural humor and quick wit, and his sincere confidence in his ability all add up to his designation as the Great Communicator. He is able to bring people over to his side in such a charming way that they don't realize they've moved until they hear themselves saying "I do." Suddenly, they're married to an idea they may not have understood before because the walk up the aisle was so convincing. (PPO/129)

□   □   □

As the press wondered why the president often left details to subordinates, no one came up with a better rationale than "that's his management style." He was born optimistic and his "can do" approach put him in the presidency. He is not a peculiar, one-of-a-kind person, as the press might make him appear. He is not "out to lunch"; he is "out to win." He has known since childhood that there is a desire in each one of us to live happily ever after and he's going to keep that little flickering flame alive in the hearts of the American people. (PPO/131)

□   □   □

Reagan's reign will be remembered for the depth of its characters, the intricacies of its plot, the many policy successes, the brilliance of its setting, the humor of its script, the resiliency of its cast, the charisma of its leading man and the conclusion we all wanted to see: "They lived happily ever after."

No one can be all things to all people, but Ronald Reagan used his strengths to their fullest and did not let his weaknesses slow him down. President Ronald Reagan, a legend in his own time, received the standing ovation of his life at the Superdome in New Orleans. As I had the exciting privilege to be among the chanting and footstomping thousands at the Republican convention, I was able to personally experience the magnetic attraction that Reagan's appearance created by his merely standing at the podium without saying a word. Here was the all-American boy with his winning smile looking down from the huge TV monitors high above the convention floor. Here was the hero we all desperately wanted, tall in the saddle, an average person who had fulfilled the American dream of becoming president. Here was the magician who took words that appeared ordinary on paper and turned them into a moving message so full of conviction, so rich in rosy images, so touching as to bring tears to thousands. Here was the master showman who with a sweep of his hand or a choke in his throat could cause chanting and applause to interrupt his forty-four-minute message sixty times. Here was the king with the passionate desire to please his subjects, waving to the beat of "Hail to the Chief," as the delegates erupted into screams and cheers while holding placards saying "Ron for King." Here was the eternal optimist lifting the hopes of his people. (PPO/132-133)

☐   ☐   ☐

Reagan will remain forever as a true representative of the Popular Personality. No matter what criticism he received he could turn it into humor, gently making fun of himself. No matter how serious his mistakes or how forgetful his mind, he could shrug his shoulders and smile and we'd be on his side.

Ronald Reagan knew how to win friends and influence people; he could keep the public's eye focusing on his strengths and quickly forgiving his weaknesses. The teflon president closed his era of peace and prosperity with the extraordinary approval rating of 60 percent. The Great Communicator came in on his strengths and with minor dips in his ratings he maintained his popularity at a remarkable level. (PPO/134)

Eleanor Roosevelt

Quiet, moody, sensitive and lonely, Perfect Eleanor was attracted to Franklin as a replica of her father's virtues without his destructive weaknesses. She transferred her sense of worship to Franklin and her insecure nature couldn't believe he would want to marry her. (PPO/39)

□　　□　　□

Eleanor pushed him and seldom let him rest. When he won his fourth term, Eleanor became almost a second president, instructing him until he had to push her away. (PPO/44)

□　　□　　□

Eleanor was able to put the hurts of [Franklin's] infidelity behind her, get beyond her lack of physical beauty and bravely march forward to become the most influential first lady we'd ever known. (PPO/45)

Franklin Roosevelt

Franklin had all the social skills of a Popular and was described as having a jaunty flirtatiousness, a winning and inspiring personality, a cavalier and regal attitude. Franklin, as a young man, loved laughter, liked to tell stories, and was the life of the party. His secondary Powerful side was his ambition, his self-discipline, his confidence, his sense of fairness and justice, and his boundless energy. (PPO/38)

□　　□　　□

FDR was Popular enough to win our support and give hope for the future, but he was also Powerful. Once in office, he showed his frightened, hungry nation that he was in charge. He was decisive, straightforward, courageous, adventurous, daring and self-confident, all traits that were sorely needed by a depressed society. (PPO/40-41)

□   □   □

FDR was passionate in his beliefs that history would prove him right, and he was willing to assume responsibility for the outcome of his programs. In order to keep his Popularity intact, FDR instituted what became known as his "Fireside Chats," informal types of radio programs where he took his problems straight to the people. (PPO/42)

□   □   □

FDR's clever use of his communication skills set him above presidents of the past and increased his Popularity to the point that he became our national father. Even those who wouldn't vote for him had to admit his personal appeal. (PPO/42)

□   □   □

Throughout his time as chief executive, FDR maintained his broad interests in life, never succumbed to self-pity, exhibited valiant energy in spite of physical debilitation, and inspired the world to admiration and respect. (PPO/43)

□   □   □

[FDR] was impatient when things didn't go his

way . . . He got angry at those who made mistakes or didn't agree with him . . . He seemed to enjoy controversy, and once said, "There is nothing I love as much as a good fight." Truly, a Powerful statement. (PPO/43)

□   □   □

While controversial, he was never boring, and in the face of attack he never lost his sense of humor. (PPO/44)

□   □   □

Of all our modern presidents, Roosevelt was the one who made the very most of his strengths, overcame his physical weaknesses, and rose above handicaps and pain.(PPO/45)

□   □   □

Compliments are food for the Populars; confidence from their troops makes them great leaders and the roar of the crowds exhilarates them. Remember how Roosevelt, sick and actually not far from death, revived and improved when he went out to the hustings on his fourth presidential campaign. Populars and Powerfuls receive strength from people, while the Peacefuls and Perfects are drained by the crowds. (PPO/118)

Harry Truman

From childhood Harry was extremely nearsighted and his wearing glasses excluded him from athletics in school. Instead he read books about heroes and leaders and by the time he was twelve he had read the Bible through twice. (PPO/48)

□ □ □

Harry learned in the military to strike first before the enemy finds you, and he carried this practice over into politics. Once he became president and emerged from the uncomfortable role as underdog with no control, he came into his own Powerful personality.

Scorned as a "little man" and a "misfit," he had a contempt for his critics that led him into impulsive actions typical of the Powerful personality . . . But Harry was buoyant, and he continued to bounce back after defeats. He had remarkable stamina and was determined to do the impossible. Being hit over the head just made him emerge taller. (PPO/49)

□ □ □

Harry's lack of finesse and his forthright phrases defined his feisty spirit, and his insecure sense of worth caused him to rattle his cage loudly and sometimes overstep his normal presidential bounds.

His strong Powerful need for control showed all too clearly when he locked horns with another Powerful, General Douglas MacArthur, who took pleasure in making policy statements without checking them with the president, for whom he had little personal respect. (PPO/50)

□ □ □

While much of the public found Harry's hot tongue and trigger-quick replies to be a humorous relief after FDR's almost god-like image, his own party cooled on his short fuse and spread the word that he would not be supported as a candidate again. (PPO/51)

POLITICS

Throughout the years as each new candidate has appeared, we have made him into an actor, endowed him with celebrity status, and put him on the stage of the political theatre. Sometimes after the choice has been made, we've become a fickle audience loving witty lines, clever turns of plot, glamorous designer costumes, low taxes and high benefits; but we've stopped applauding when our hero brought depression, war, civil unrest, scandal, apathy, hostages, and the Ayatollah onto the stage. (PPO/13)

□　□　□

Since the Declaration of Independence, the Powerfuls have been influential politicians. Because of their innate desire to lead, they took to political office like the proverbial duck to water. Imagine a whole district to dominate, a whole state to sublimate, a whole country to control! (PPO/22)

□　□　□

Throughout history, the Populars have been drawn into politics because it combines talk and work, promises and patronage, personality and position, con-

217

fidence and charm. (PPO/19)

□   □   □

The Perfects didn't intend to be politicians—the whole system seems so unsystematic; yet as they looked at the shallow intellect of the available candidates, they felt a self-sacrificing call to save the nation from the collection of nit-wits trying to lead it nowhere in a hurry. Once involved, the Perfects couldn't leave the political parties unperfected, and they felt deeply about the punctuation of the platforms and the construction of the constitution.

The Perfects were brought up in ivory towers, giving them a somewhat unrealistic view of the masses below. They believe in the basic goodness of each individual and idealistically look to the day when the slums are slammed shut, the castles closed up, and we all live happily ever after in the suburbs. (PPO/26)

□   □   □

The Peacefuls didn't intend to go into politics as it appears fraught with difficulties, conflicts and stress, and demands decisions, new ideas, and endless effort. Since they aren't flashy people and tend to resist responsibility, they didn't want to be in charge of anything, but often they won by default, they became the compromise candidate. Their greatest strength was their lack of obvious weaknesses. The Peacefuls weren't noted for innovative legislation but for healing the hurts and binding the wounds. (PPO/30)

□   □   □

Could we create the perfect candidate? One who looks like Paul Newman, speaks like Charleton Heston, promotes family values like Bill Cosby, is morally spotless like Mr. Clean, is a TV natural like Johnny Carson, sings like Paul Simon, and is revered internationally like Ronald McDonald?

Is there such a person? Can we ever find a Superman sitting on a pot of gold at the end of our romantic rainbow?

We want the Shakespearean hero without the tragic flaw. (PPO/140)

□   □   □

The reason that the Kennedy and Reagan regimes have been described as reigns, Camelots and Kingdoms, is that the rulers looked like kings. They both presented themselves as royalty, were ruggedly handsome on first glance, and had magnetic appeal that riveted attention. Each one came with a real queen who wore designer gowns, ate from gold-rimmed plates every day, and maintained a regal air of confidence even in drastic situations. (PPO/155)

□   □   □

When politicians first appeared on television, what you saw was what they were. The individual candidates came on live without being cleaned up, cosmeticized, or coached. If the suit was wrinkled, the hair wind-blown, or the tie crooked, we accepted that as a

219

part of the vicissitudes of everyday life.

Media managers and image consultants came bursting forth to make candidates camera ready. What a shame these fairy godmothers had not been around earlier to replace George Washington's wooden false teeth and camouflage President Taft's weight problems. (PPO/156)

□   □   □

With this chorus line of candidates costumed and cued, how can we ever know what each one is really like when off the political stage? The answer is that we can't really know them; some of their mates may not really know them. We may see them on camera more often than their children see them at home. By watching the candidates, or any public person, however, we can get a sense of their personalities through their gestures, postures and responses. As we observe debates, forums and interviews on TV, we can see how each person reacts to attacks and whether or not he has a sense of humor, or any sense at all. We can see how they voted on issues that represent our values, thereby knowing with some accuracy how they will vote in the future. (PPO/157)

□   □   □

Up until the time of Kennedy, religion was seldom an issue in politics. Candidates were assumed to be respectable citizens who went to church regularly and their spiritual values weren't questioned. With the strong Irish Catholic beliefs of the Kennedys came a fear that the Pope might end up in the White House in some kind of an advisory position, a fear that never materialized.

During the time of Richard Nixon, reared as a Quaker, Billy Graham was brought into the White House to preach and counsel. A personal faith was openly talked about, but the unsavory end to the Nixon regime dimmed any spiritual influence that Graham might have had.

Gerald Ford talked of a Christian commitment but evangelicals winced at Betty's strong stand for the Equal Rights Amendment. Jimmy Carter brought the term "Born Again" into the political arena, gave his personal conversion testimony and taught Sunday school in a Baptist church. Ronald Reagan fought for conservative Christian causes and reversed many liberal trends . . . and Episcopalian George Bush passed the spiritual test when questioned in *Christianity Today*. (PPO/167-168)

PRAYER

As the incense burned on the altar and ascended to God, so our prayers start in the heart and reach up to heaven when we pray in the power of our intercessor, when we pray "in Jesus' name." (LFG/227)

□   □   □

We must be alert and not let the fire within us go out. We don't want to be lukewarm Christians whose pitiful prayers never get above our heads. (LFG/228)

□   □   □

Our earnest prayers waft as incense up to the

221

heavenly Father. How He loves to smell the aroma as we worship Him in prayer. We can then feel His power and know there will be wonderful results. (LFG/230)

□ □ □

Do you really believe that God knows you? Do you believe that He knows the hairs on your head? Do you believe that not a sparrow falls without His knowing? The Bible assures us that God knows His children. A father wants the best for his family and will give his children all he has.

Sometimes we ask for things that are wrong and wonder why we don't receive them, but our Father God knows our needs and He knows our future. If our children ask permission to go to a party where drugs are available, we do them no favor by allowing them to go. So it is with our heavenly Father. He knows what's best for us. (AEW/95)

□ □ □

Why is it that you men should dwell with your wife according to spiritual knowledge of marriage, give honor to her, and be her loving leader? You do this in order "that your prayers be not hindered" (1 Peter 3:7). Conversely, if you don't follow the instructions in this verse you cannot expect to have a very effective prayer life. (AEW/112)

□ □ □

Why is there a renewed interest in prayer? The

reason is that all else has failed. In this country we have believed in ourselves and our ability to rise from nothing to greatness. We started as an odd collection of pilgrims seeking religious freedom and fugitives from the law of other countries. Like a child who has run away from home, we wanted to show our Father we could make it on our own. With many struggles we grew up and we became the greatest. The United States of America has been on top with its form of government, its military, its resources, its education, its morals, its families, its individuals. When you're the best, you don't need outside help. (ITS/177)

□   □   □

How do you pray ABOVE AVERAGE? You remember the prodigal son who had "wasted his substance on riotous living" and then "came to himself" and returned home. He didn't bring a big list of requests, he just came to the gate with a humble and contrite heart.

How about you? Have you been praying below average prayers? Have you been asking for favors, presenting conditions or calling for help when you're still in the far country? Come home. Come home! (ITS/179)

□   □   □

How many people do you know who pray for you daily? How many are uplifting you and praising God for your very existence? How many do you pray for consistently? Do you let them know how much you care?

Can you bring yourself to pray for problem people? Can you pray for those who've hurt you?

Paul shows genuine concern for Philemon and adds in verse 6:

"My prayer is that our fellowship with you as believers will bring about a deeper understanding of every blessing which we have in our life in union with Christ" (TEV).

Paul longs for a "deeper understanding." Paul really cares, even as God cares for you and me. (GAD/123)

PROBLEMS

The reason more of us don't turn to the Bible in times of trouble is that we don't know where to look for the answers. (BBC/96)

□   □   □

I used to think that every woman with a problem wanted an answer. I assumed that if I threw out a solution to a man, he would snap it up and run home with it tucked under his arm, eager to put it into play. In fact, I was so sure that all troubled people would jump for my remedies that I originally wrote my lessons on marriage without the first step, DECIDE if you want to improve the situation.

But the more I worked with real-live people with real-live problems, the more I began to see how few wanted to do something to improve the situation. I soon realized that if they couldn't grab hold of number 1 and decide to take action no matter what the partner did, there was no point in bothering with the rest of the steps at all. I found I could lay out brilliant plans for a life, but if the person before me had no desire to move, the thoughts and the time were wasted. So often a person is unwilling to take the first step until he sees that his partner is underway. Consequently, neither one improves and they sit in a series of stalemates. (AEW/80-81)

□　□　□

Sometimes we have to get between a rock and a hard place to look sincerely for our God, but like Jacob, we too can meet God on the rocks. (LFG/76)

□　□　□

Joseph continued his intimate relationship with God while in prison — he walked with God in the darkness as well as in the light . . . Are our circumstances so much worse than Joseph's that we can't trust God to redeem us? (LFG/96-98)

□　□　□

As we reflect on our lives, we see that we have each had a beginning, each fallen into some kind of trouble, each tried to find a way out. Just as the Hebrews in Egyptian slavery were trying to escape, so are we seeking solutions for our problems. As they were looking for a savior, so we are looking for a God who'll set us free. (LFG/109)

□　□　□

There are many avenues which we can pursue to

gain greater understanding of the problems we face. The outside help we find is a tool in God's hands to encourage us or give us deeper insight. However, the ultimate answer always rests in His Word and in the transforming love of God. (BBC/95)

□   □   □

If I had written the Bible I would have put things differently: I would have given each committed believer an easy life. But God did not see it my way; He planned life on earth to be a testing ground for our future. As a parent toward a child he loves, God chastens us for our own good. He allows us to go through trials to perfect our character. (BBC/101-102)

□   □   □

We don't need to squirm out of our difficulties, but face them, knowing that God is faithful and that He will not allow us to be tested too far. He does not promise us a rose garden, but He does say that with the trial He will provide us a way of escape. When I first read that word "escape" I was encouraged. God was going to help me run away from my problems, skirt around them, or tunnel under them; but then I looked at the last clause: "that you may be able to bear it." To bear anything you have to stay with it. These thoughts seemed contradictory, so I hunted up the word "escape" in its original use and found that it means to be lifted above the problem enough to get a more detached perspective. This escape is what God has for us: He will pick us up from the depth of our depression and give us an objective view of our situation so that we will be able to bear it, not run away from it. (BBC/102)

PRUNING

Picture yourself as a rosebush. You have produced flowers in the past, but God the Gardener knows you could blossom even more. To make you bloom to your full potential, to make you a blue-ribbon winner, He must prune off all that's keeping you from the prize. Let's review the pruning principles and see how they relate to us.

1. Pruning is not punishment but purposeful planning. God is not cutting you to hurt you, but to produce perfection.

2. God the Gardener already has in mind what He wants you to look like. He has a plan for your ultimate use and only He has the picture of the finished product. When you get rebuffed in one area, stopped in one pursuit, cut by a friend, God knows it hurts but He knows it is necessary to bring you into His purposeful planning, to shape you like that open vessel.

3. When God, who holds the blueprint, gazes down upon us, He sees branches that are sticking out with no rhyme or reason, pursuits in our life that are without eternal values, selfish goals that detract from our spiritual shape. He needs to cut these off, but since He doesn't stroll around our garden with big pruning shears, He sends people to do it for Him, friends who tell us things "for our own good," mates who point out how much time we're wasting, mothers-in-law who show us how they did it better. Some bushes don't take this pruning kindly and they never bear much fruit. Some accept

the cuts, learn from the comments, and go on to win the prizes.

4. Since God's purpose is to produce an open vessel ready to be filled with His Holy Spirit, He needs to empty out all that's cluttering up our lives. He sees branches that are rubbing against each other causing friction in our relationships and He has to clip them out. He sees activities that are at cross-purposes keeping us busy in all directions but achieving little. He sees projects that are positive but are pulling us away from His plan. He sees anger, bitterness, jealousy and other negative emotions which are choking out our spiritual air so we are gasping for breath. He sends His saints with His scissors to shape us up and sometimes we refuse to be shorn.

5. Have you ever watched a sucker shoot grow? Recently I had one that touched the roof. One week it wasn't there and the next week it was ten feet high. It shot off in a flash, using up every ounce of strength the poor bush had. Healthy leaves shriveled up and buds drooped their little heads. Often we beautiful rosebushes allow sucker shoots to run rampant. We have projects, problems, or pressures that take over our lives, grow out of control and drain our energy dry. Unpruned, these shoots so sap our strength that we have no stamina left. God the Gardener knows a sucker shoot when He sees one and He sends His angels to warn us that we're springing off in the wrong direction, that we need to call a quick halt to this unproductive growth.

6. As God trains His little helpers who come to clip us, He asks them to use sharp shears so we won't be torn up in the process of pruning. However, as with every profession in life, some are slow learners and inflict more pain than others. But once we accept God's program—

Pruning is not punishment but purposeful planning — we can absorb the cutting cheerfully and ultimately ask for it. (ITS/44-45)

☐   ☐   ☐

When God sends His workers they will be there not for punishment but for purposeful planning. So the next time you look up and see that lady approaching who loves to cut you down, smile cheerfully, ask for her advice, and pray that her shears are sharp. (ITS/46)

R

REDEMPTION

In Matthew 18:15-17 the Lord Jesus gives four steps in redeeming, not condemning, the person at fault.

1. Go to him privately and hope to win him back.

2. If he won't listen, take one or two other people with you as witnesses.

3. If he still won't listen, take the matter before the church (presumably the board of elders or deacons).

4. If he won't listen to the church, remove him from the fellowship.

Before you go to straighten out the other person, remember that the Lord also said, "Let him without sin cast the first stone." (GAD/81)

RELIGION

Fred's and my differences in religion, coupled with our double tragedy, split us apart and left us with no faith at all. (AEW/17).

□   □   □

Never have there been so many diverse groups

claiming to have kidnaped God and to be keeping Him exclusively for their adherents. (LFG/34)

□   □   □

Recently the president of a seminary told me he had done a survey on the adult children of his denomination's leaders and pastors and found a startling figure; only 20 percent of these children were still "in church." Obviously, these young adults who were brought up in the church were so turned off by what they saw and lived through that they wanted no part of institutional religion when they were out on their own. (RTC/176)

□   □   □

How great it would be if the church worked to prevent problems instead of reacting in shock when they happen. (BBC/191)

False Religion

One desperate lady cried out to me, "I've tried everything—even transgressional medication!" Little did she realize in her mistaken memory of her transcendental meditation experience that her misnomer was what she needed: a soothing medicine to eliminate her transgressions! (LFG/27)

□   □   □

If you or a friend are at all doubtful about any

231

group or practice you are considering, ask yourself these questions:

In this group, is a certain person, whether living or dead, revered and honored above the Lord Jesus? Someone like Jim Jones, Rev. Moon, the Rajneesh, or some spirit speaking through a human being? "Salvation is found in no one else, for there is no other name under heaven given to men by which we must be saved" (Acts 4:12, NIV).

Does a person or practice exert control over your mind or your money and dictate what you must do or give? "For the love of money is a root of all kinds of evil. Some people, eager for money, have wandered from the faith and pierced themselves with many griefs" (1 Timothy 6:10, NIV).

Is prosperity considered to be a means to or sign of spiritual success? Does the leader promote sacrificial giving and yet seem to live a lavish lifestyle personally?

Do individuals attempt to shift you into a state where they are in control of your bodily movements or emotions? Do you notice any members who seem to be in a trance or dazed condition? Any who are kept apart from the main group for periods of time?

Are there any moral or ethical practices contrary to what you know God would expect of you? Examples: Go out and have an affair; it will lower your stress level. Steal from the rich and give to the poor. The Bible tells us in Ephesians that we are to behave in accordance with the truth that is in Jesus. "Be made new in the attitude of your minds; . . . put on the new self, created to be like God in true righteousness and holiness" (4:23,24, NIV).

Are there books or other printed materials that are considered inspired and held above the Bible in importance? "But even if we or an angel from heaven should preach a gospel other than the one we preached to you, let him be eternally condemned!" (Galatians 1:8, NIV).

Are the rules, practices, preachings, and theories of this group or religion inconsistent with the Word of God? "The things that come out of the mouth come from the heart, and these make a man 'unclean.' . . . evil thoughts, murder, adultery, sexual immorality, theft, false testimony, slander" (Matthew 15:18-19, NIV).

Do spirit and sex seem to go hand in hand? Is any kind of free sex advocated or accepted? Does the leader exempt himself from normal moral principles? "Thou shalt not commit adultery" (Exodus 20:14, KJV).

Is getting drunk, drugged, or high a part of the ritual and considered a sign of spirituality? "And be not drunk with wine, wherein is excess; but be filled with the Spirit" (Ephesians 5:18, KJV).

To belong to this group, do you have to change the style of your dress or hair? Do you have to move to some separate area? Forsake family and friends?

Are you encouraged to get in touch with your past lives or dead relatives? "And as it is appointed unto men once to die, but after this the judgment" (Hebrews 9:27, KJV).

Do the members use mediums, cards, boards, crystal balls, love crystals, or any other implements or spirits to get close to God? Leviticus 19:31 cautions: "Do not defile yourselves by consulting mediums and wizards, for I am Jehovah your God" (TLB).

If any of your answers to this check list are yes, I

233

suggest that you locate some respected Christian leader outside of the group you are considering and ask for counsel before you get involved. All kinds of new religions have sprung up and many initially seem to be warm, loving, sincere, Christian groups. We must all be very careful that in our search for God, we don't end up in the wrong places. (LFG/34-36)

RESPECT

When Freddie was about ten years old he yelled some nasty comment to me. Fred reached over to him, grabbed him by the shoulders, picked him up off the ground, and shook him hard. "Don't you ever let me hear you say one bad word to my wife again!" And he plunked him down. Freddie got the message quickly and clearly. He was never to say anything like that to me again! And he didn't. If you have a Choleric son you may have to grab him often and shake him harder, but he will soon get the idea that you do not tolerate any disrespect for your wife. Give honor to your wife and make sure that your children do also. (AEW/110)

□   □   □

Since God commands that we honor our parents, is there any hope that we can fellowship with God and know His power if we are not showing honor to our parents and are allowing our own children to be disrespectful toward us? (LFG/151)

□   □   □

If you have no spirit of honor for your parents and you aren't taught differently, you have no respect for life. (LFG/152)

ROMANCE

The media makes us think that a male's appeal lies mainly in his manly physique, seductive glances, gold chains, and costly cologne. While these attributes may enhance the chase, it takes more than a front to keep romance in a marriage. When a wife has been insulted or ignored, she won't be impressed by a quick flash of Aramis or muscles that were toned up by a body-building course. (AEW/128)

S

SALVATION

My sister-in-law Ruthie took me to a Christian Women's Club. I didn't want to go and I didn't intend to listen to the speaker; yet, when a tall, distinguished gentleman stood up, I listened. He told a story of a woman like me who was unhappy. She was a good person who even went to church, but she didn't know how to receive spiritual power in her life. I didn't either.

The speaker quoted Romans 12:1,2: "Present your bodies a living sacrifice, holy, acceptable unto God, which is your reasonable service. And be not conformed to this world, but be transformed by the renewing of your mind, that ye may prove what is that good and acceptable and perfect will of God for you." I had heard this before, but, as with all my Bible knowledge, it didn't mean anything to me personally. He said there might be ladies in the audience who needed help, and I nodded my head.

Then these thoughts came through to me. *I should present my body. I should give myself away. To whom? To God through Jesus Christ.* I had already given up on myself, so now I had to give myself away to the Lord Jesus. "Why not?" I thought. "I'm a failure anyway. Why keep me around?"

I didn't think I was giving away much of a prize, nor did I think the Lord was going to be too excited to add one more gloomy girl to His group. I decided to donate myself anyway.

Be not conformed to the world. I had spent my life working on worldly standards. I had planned a career in teaching followed by a perfect marriage and perfect children. I wanted to live up to the best standards the world had to offer. I had such good motives, yet I had produced two brain-damaged sons and the world had no answers. Conforming to the world had not helped me, so what had I to lose?

Be transformed. The verse told me that when I gave myself to the Lord and quit worrying about the world, God would transform me. How I needed a change, a new life! How I needed to get beyond my personal gloom to a higher plane! How I needed more than the happy pills the doctors had offered! God promised to renew my mind, I was ready to take Him up on it.

Know God's will. Then you will know (how I needed to be sure of something!) what is that good, acceptable, and perfect will of God for you. I didn't think God even knew me. I surely had never known Him in a personal way, but I was willing to become acquainted with any power that could transform me from hopelessness to health, that could give me a new mind and a new direction.

I prayed right there in that restaurant. Religion needs the ritual of a church, but a spiritual relationship can start in a restaurant. I asked Jesus Christ to come into my life and give me a new mind. I also asked that He show me clearly what God's plan for my discouraged life should be.

Once I made this commitment to the Lord I felt better. For the first time I knew I was a Christian, not because I wasn't something else but because I had given myself to Christ. (BBC/98-100)

□　　□　　□

Many people fear that in giving their lives to God He will present them with a big list of don'ts and their fun will be over. I found that He doesn't give don'ts but changes desires. (BBC/103)

□　　□　　□

As man approached God in the Old Testament tabernacle at the altar, we can come close to God in only one way through His son Jesus Christ—"He that hath seen me hath seen the father" (John 14:9). To go through the Gate of the Christian life and step toward the presence of the Father, we must pay the price, bring an offering, make a sacrifice. (LFG/191)

□　　□　　□

We may be religious and refer to the Lord as our friend, but if we've never been dropped to our knees by the overwhelming power of His majesty, if we've never taken our shoes off because we know we're on His holy ground, perhaps we've never found the real God, the King of Kings. (LFG/112)

□　　□　　□

Looking for God takes more than an hour on Sunday. It requires disciplined dedication and the desire to be content in the desert. (LFG/174)

□   □   □

When I first found that Jesus was the link between the old and new covenants, suddenly the whole Bible came together and made sense. Jesus wasn't a latter-day idea, but the embodiment of the Old Testament signs and symbols. The tabernacle wasn't just an old tent in the desert, but the figure of our everlasting home in the heavenlies. (LFG/182)

□   □   □

As there was one way into the courts of God in Moses' time, there is today one way, one door, into the presence of God. (LFG/184)

□   □   □

As we start coming out of our desert experience and start seeking God, we must realize there is a barrier between us and God. But God has provided an open entrance: Jesus Christ the Way, the Truth, and the Life. There is no back door to God, but a gate with a bright light waiting for us to enter His courts with praise.

Many of us, however, stand around the door knowing that it's there, but not quite wanting to go in. We view the door as some kind of a fire-escape; when the flames come we know where to run. For those of us who have been pulling ourselves out of Egypt, wandering in the wilderness, and hoping to find God, just knowing where the door is and what it looks like and perhaps

239

touching the doorpost is not enough. We have to make a decision. Do we want to go inside or not? Are we ready to make a commitment to the Lord Jesus? He is our door, our gate, our way. Have we come this far to turn back? Are we content to be an outsider? Are we going to hover around the door and make a run for it at the last minute?

Let's not wait. Let's make that commitment to our Lord now so that we can enter into His courts with praise.

"Commit your way to the Lord; trust in him" (Psalm 37:5, NIV).

Here is a sample prayer of commitment.

Dear Jesus, I've been looking for God in some odd places and now I'm standing at Your door. I see that I'll never get near to God until I pass through this door. I accept that You are the way, the truth, and the life and that I can't come to God except through You. I make a personal commitment to You and ask that You will open the gate that I might come in to the very presence of God.

I pray this in the name of Jesus. Amen. (LFG/185)

□   □   □

Although the gate to salvation is wide, the door to God's presence is small, only large enough for those who have already given their lives to Jesus our Lord who proclaimed, "Enter through the narrow gate. For wide is the gate and broad is the road that leads to destruction, and many enter through it. But small is the gate and narrow the road that leads to life, and only a few find it" (Matthew 7:13,14, NIV). (LFG/218)

□   □   □

What an amazing book the Bible is! How perfectly the Word of God constructed the Old Testament and the tabernacle and brought it all together in the New Testament and the Lord Jesus Christ. Could anyone but God have woven these plans and predictions into a whole cloth and then placed the mantle on you and me that we might stand in His presence. (LFG/243)

□   □   □

When we find God, others will notice the change. Not only will we look more radiant as we reflect the Lord's glory, but also the Holy Spirit, the power and energy of the trinity, will transform us into the likeness of Christ. Bit by bit there will be changes as we commit our lives to Jesus and obey His will for us.

We will begin to manifest the fruit of the Spirit. As we stand in the presence of God we will have more *love* for others than we ever thought was possible. We will be able to exhibit the *joy* of the Lord even in adverse circumstances. The *peace* that passes all understanding will keep our hearts and minds safe in Christ Jesus. *Patience* that we never had will come over us in a wave of compassion and understanding for those we could barely tolerate before. An attitude of relaxed *kindness* to others will replace our self-seeking natures, and a real *goodness*, a true desire to help without thought of human credit, will become apparent to those we meet. For some of us who have wavered in our dedication to God in the past, the gift of *faithfulness* will be added, and people will see that we've been with Jesus. There will be a new *gentleness*, a softness in our face and in our actions that will

241

attract people to us, and we will gain *self-control* over some of our habits and tempers that have hindered others from seeking the Lord. (LFG/244)

□   □   □

We may not see the Father face to face until the day He calls us to His eternal home. But we know we are in His presence when we accept the gift He has placed before us—the gift of His Son who died that we might be put right with our Father God. Yes, Jesus gave Himself for us that we might stand before God with nothing left against us. And when we accept His gift, we are acquitted; we're not guilty; we are free! (LFG/247)

□   □   □

What a guarantee we have in our Christian faith that God is always at work in us to make us willing and able to obey His purpose; to tax the last limit of the universe to help us take the right road. Yet He's not there to do our work but to equip us to do it. He's not a giant genie in the sky available to do magic tricks when we call on Him, but He will help us to take the right road. (FYM/70)

SANGUINES/POPULARS

The Populars started out in life with winning ways. The little girls knew how to charm their fathers and the boys knew how to roll their eyes toward mother. They talked early and constantly, said adorable things and seemed to attract doting attention. They managed to delight their teachers, gather a retinue of little friends, become class president and be voted the most likely to succeed. They starred in the Senior Class Play, became flamboyant athletes and cheerleaders, and were the life of every party. As adults they aimed at professions that emphasized glamour over work, creativity over routines, loose hours over schedules, and people over statistics. With their appealing personalities they were promoted quickly until they reached a plateau where more than an easygoing performance was required for advancement. (PPO/18)

□   □   □

Fred and I were once at a party where a delightful Sanguine girl named Bonnie enthralled the group with her detailed description of a boat trip from Los Angeles to Catalina Island. She relived the entertainment for us all, recited the menu, told who got seasick, and held our attention for twenty minutes. As soon as she concluded her hilarious story about their boat trip to Catalina, her Melancholy husband took a deep breath and said, quietly but firmly, two words: *We flew.*

We all stood stunned as Bonnie reflected for a moment and then agreed, "That's right, we flew."

Only a Sanguine could spend twenty minutes describing in detail a trip she'd never taken on a boat she'd never boarded.

Although the Sanguines' stories are funny and I'll never forget this incident, Bonnie had gone so far in her exaggerations that she was lying. A friend told me a similar situation this morning and concluded with "Of course she's a Sanguine, so you can't believe a word she says." Isn't that a shame? Isn't it too bad Sanguines can't be trusted to deal anywhere near the truth? Think it over and check yourself. (PPL/92-93)

□   □   □

While the Sanguine stories are funny, they show that the Sanguine means well but seldom reaches his potential. He doesn't want to get down to work today. Something always comes up. Pleasure outranks work. (PPL/101-102)

□   □   □

The Sanguines have the creative ability to take their obvious weaknesses and find ways to turn them into strengths. (PPL/97)

□   □   □

Give Sanguines an audience and they'll start a script. (PPL/32)

□   □   □

All Sanguines need good, quiet Phlegmatic friends! (PPL/79)

□   □   □

The Sanguine's great ability to carry on a colorful conversation whether in the Co-op or the Congo is a plus envied by others; *but* carried to extremes, the Sanguine is constantly talking, monopolizing, and interrupting. (PPL/83)

□   □   □

A Sanguine pastor I know often gets so excited over his sermon that he feels encumbered with one hand holding the Bible and only one free for waving, so he rises up and down on his toes and makes emphatic points with a kick of one foot. If you don't happen to be fascinated with his subject matter, you will be enthralled, watching to see how long he can do this jig without losing his balance. (PPL/33)

□   □   □

One girl described her Sanguine family by saying, "We grew up in a house where emotions were dripping off the wall." (PPL/33)

□   □   □

The word extraordinary must have been created to describe Sanguines because their every thought and word is way beyond the ordinary and is definitely extra. Miss Piggy hit on a Sanguine truth when she said in her fashion tips, "Too much is never enough." (PPL/33)

□   □   □

One night as Fred and I were teaching temperaments to a group in New York, I mentioned how

Sanguines volunteer and don't follow through. "For example," I said, "if a Sanguine had volunteered to make the coffee for our break tonight, we would find that she had forgotten even to plug in the pot." At that point, an adorable, bright-eyed girl in the front row screamed, ran up the aisle, and disappeared into the kitchen. She was Sanguine; she had volunteered to make the coffee, she had never plugged in the pot, and we had nothing to drink that night. Sanguines love to volunteer, and they mean well, but if you want coffee, you'd better plug it in yourself! (PPL/35)

□   □   □

Because the Sanguines have an abundance of energy and enthusiasm, they tend to attract and inspire others. Harry Truman once said that leadership is the ability to inspire others to work and make them enjoy doing it. This statement sums up the Sanguines and shows their subtle style of leadership. The effective Sanguine thinks up the ideas and charms others into carrying them out to a productive conclusion. As a Sanguine begins to understand himself, he realizes he is a starter, but he needs friends who are finishers. (PPL/36)

□   □   □

The Sanguines are the life-of-the-party, colorful, exciting people, with a sense of humor. They have charisma, innate charm, and a magnetic personality. However, they talk too much, want all the attention to be on themselves, seldom follow through on what they start, and don't often achieve their full potential. Their aim is to have fun out of life. Their compulsion is to entertain the troops. They usually marry Melancholies to bring order into their lives, and when their mate tries to organize them they rebel. (GAD/37)

□   □   □

Don't criticize [a Sanguine] and tell him to improve, even though that seems logical. Sanguines are desperate for praise, and negative words may well paralyze any positive action.

Compliment him on his ability to get along with people and ask how he ever accomplishes so much in a given day.

At this point any fun-loving Sanguine is ready for you to offer assistance. If you don't precede the offer with the proper build-up, the Sanguine will refuse help because it's very important that he not lose face or appear incompetent. (GAD/44-45)

□   □   □

Sanguines need quiet help done in such a way that they get the credit. (GAD/46)

□   □   □

A Sanguine wants to be popular, and she's found that being the dispenser of deceptive details puts her in the center of the action.

Much as you may want to, you don't start off by calling her a liar, but you also must make sure you don't play her games.

Don't tell her anything you don't want published.

Neither give nor listen to "secrets."

Don't pass on anything she says.

When she talks about happenings, ask "Were you there?"

When she tells about people, ask "Have you told them?"

When you have a chance to share with her, say, "You have such an entertaining way of speaking and such a gift for communicating that there's no need for you to exaggerate. Fact is always stranger than fiction." Follow this up with an invitation to do something fun, and let her know you like her for herself. She doesn't need to confide secrets—you like her as she is. (GAD/47)

□   □   □

Whatever the Sanguine says, it will be exaggerated and exuberant, and you won't have any trouble hearing it. Once you spot the Sanguine, you can make a quick decision. If you want to be entertained, stay. If you want to talk yourself, quickly flee to another room and find a sedentary Phlegmatic who will listen. (PPL/163)

□   □   □

More than any other temperament, Sanguines are controlled by their circumstances. Their emotions go up and down according to what is happening around them. When you realize how quickly their emotions change, you won't overreact to their hysteria. It's unfortunate for the Sanguines that they cry "Wolf!" too often. One lady told me she leaned over a gas burner and her sleeve caught on fire. She screamed to her husband in the other room, "Help! Help! I'm on fire!" and he called back, "You sure are, honey. You're hot stuff!" (PPL/171)

Sanguine/Popular Parent

The Popular Parent loves to have fun and thrives on an audience. Often the children become the audience and the Sanguine mother will really turn on her stage personality when a group of little friends arrive who think she's so much more entertaining than their own mother. As long as the Popular mother gets attention, she will play games with the children, but since the Sanguines all get their self-worth from the response of those around them, a disinterested group will cause them to turn off their charm. Why bother being cute and adorable if no one cares. (RTC/36)

□   □   □

Ever the showman, the Popular Parent would like to have the starring role and have an eternal position on center stage without being responsible for any of the hard work or details. Responsibility is not a plus in the Popular Parent's mind and frequently the other personalities call them air-heads. However, the mistakes they make that would embarrass others become fascinating material for their ever-growing reservoir of entertaining stories.

A light-hearted, possibly light-headed, Popular personality from Phoenix wrote me this story. If it had happened to a more serious person it would have been buried away in a box forever:

249

"My husband's nephew had his sixth birthday and I had gotten a darling tooth pillow for him to use after he pulled a tooth. Well, I boxed it all up, gift-wrapped it, and mailed it to Tennessee and was very proud of the 'different' gift I had sent. Later they called and said there was nothing in the box and they wondered what happened. Poor Aaron had looked and looked but found nothing. I couldn't figure out what happened as I even remembered putting the pillow in the box. Sure enough, back in the hall closet *in a box* was the pillow. Somehow I had mailed the wrong one! An empty one!"

This kind of a mother is most appreciated by children of a similar personality who can laugh along with them. (RTC/36)

□   □   □

Popular Parents will enjoy the strengths of the high-achieving Powerful children, brag about their achievements, and share the spotlight in any honors. The problem comes when the child, sensing the parent's lack of resolve and follow-through, takes control of the parent's life, dictates the time when they wish to be picked up, and reprimands the parent for being late. (RTC/37)

□   □   □

Popular Parents will have the least understanding for their Perfect Melancholy children who don't respond well to their parents' bubbling humor. Since response is what Popular Parents need, this deeply intuitive child makes an inner decision not to give them what they want. They take secret pleasure in their quiet power to unnerve mother by refusing to applaud her antics. My Melancholy son once said, "It's amazing that people pay money to hear you speak. I guess that's because they don't have to listen to you for nothing." (RTC/38)

□　　□　　□

Popular Parents will enjoy the relaxed, unpressured attitude of the Peaceful Phlegmatic child, but will be disappointed when this child refuses to get excited over their numerous brilliant ideas. The more the Popular Parent pushes for energetic enthusiasm, the more stubborn this child will become. The two share a mutual disinterest in organization and they both are casual about appointments and time, but the differences become apparent in the area of enthusiasm. The Popular Parent lives for excitement and the Peaceful child wants to avoid it. The Popular Parent loves noise and confusion, the Peaceful child wants it quiet. Another conflict comes in the area of decision making. The Popular Parent loves to do things on the spur of the moment, while the Peaceful child has difficulty in making decisions in the best of times and becomes traumatized when an excited parent pushes for an instant decision. (RTC/41-42)

Sanguine-Choleric

The Sanguine-Choleric combination is a natural blend. They are both outgoing, optimistic, and outspoken. The Sanguine talks for pleasure, the Choleric for business, but they both are verbal people. If you have this blend, you have the greatest potential for leadership. If you combine your two strengths, you have a person who can direct others and make them enjoy the work; a person who is fun-loving, yet can accomplish goals; a person with drive and determination, but not compulsive about achievements. This blend takes the extremes of work and play and produces a person who puts them in proper perspective. In the negative, such a blend could spawn a bossy individual who didn't know what he was talking about; an impulsive person who was running around in circles; or an impatient soul who was always interrupting and monopolizing conversation. (PPL/141)

□ □ □

To get along positively with the positive Sanguine-Choleric person who carries positive thinking to extremes, we should realize that it is their single-mindedness of purpose that has made them successful in life. (GAD/94)

Sanguine-Phlegmatic

The other complementary blend is the Sanguine-Phlegmatic. Where the Choleric-Melancholy is work oriented, the Sanguine-Phlegmatic is inclined to take it easy and have fun. The combination of double portions of humor with easygoing natures makes the Sanguine-Phlegmatics the best friends possible. Their warm, relaxed natures are appealing and people love to be with them. The Phlegmatic tempers the ups and downs of the Sanguine, while the Sanguine personality brightens up the Phlegmatic. This blend is the best of all in dealing with people. They are good in personnel work, in being parents, and in civic leadership, because they have the engaging humor and personality of the Sanguine and the stability of the Phlegmatic. Unfortunately, the other side of the Sanguine-Phlegmatic shows them as lazy, without desire or direction to produce anything they can avoid. As with each temperament blend there are exciting strengths and corresponding weaknesses. (PPL/144)

SELF-CENTEREDNESS

Isn't it amazing that when we remove God, consider Him dead, and seek our own ways, morals and human decency soon come tumbling after? (LFG/157)

☐ ☐ ☐

During the 70's we went through what was called the "me generation." We were told that it was time to think of ourselves, examine our psyche, and do our own thing. We were to throw old-fashioned morals and principles aside (because they had been holding us down) and instead develop our full potential.

We've spent ten years learning to look out for number one, but all we came up with was people who no longer made an effort to get along with anyone else. It's always the other person's fault. If you don't like the way I function, then get out. So people have gotten out. The family is no longer a group trying for some kind of unity and harmony, but separate individuals who for a time are living under the same roof. Everyone is working for the luxuries that we now see as necessities, and the children are being brought up in day care centers. "Latchkey Kids" is a new expression used for the thousands of children who come home to an empty house and are free to "do their own thing" until dinnertime. (GAD/101-102)

SELF-IMPROVEMENT

We start all our seminars with a quick examination of the temperaments because we have found this to be the most effective tool for self-examination. We can see our strengths and weaknesses so clearly, and because it's done on a group level, we don't feel threatened individually.

Look over the temperament charts and find three of your weaknesses that you know need to be changed, and set to work on them. Remember, you Sanguines are quick to admit that you have some minor faults and to apologize for them, but underneath you think they are really trivial matters and you're not concerned enough or disciplined enough to act on them.

You Cholerics don't think you really have any faults. You have proven over the years that if everyone else would do what you tell them to do when you tell them to do it, everything would go just fine. You have great difficulty in believing that your perfect behavior and instructions could possibly be offensive to others—but they are!

You Melancholies get easily depressed when you look at all the things wrong with you. It's too much; there's no hope. But that's not true. You are most able of all temperaments to accept your weaknesses and to systematically get to work on self-improvement. Choose only three areas; you know that you and the Lord can do it.

You Phlegmatics admit that you have some flaws, but you've managed to get along so far without having to do much about them. Other people have done your work and you're so easy to get along with that you've never been pushed into change. Are you willing now to look at three areas of weakness (or at least one or two) and force yourself to do something about them? Stand up now, flex your muscles, and let's move! (AEW/87)

□   □   □

The first step in any type of self-improvement is to find your areas of weakness and admit you have them. The refusal to examine our faults keeps us from doing anything positive about them. It is humbling to admit we've been doing something wrong for years, but it's the first step in growing up. Immature people blame their parents, their mates, their children, their friends, their circumstances, for why they have not become what they had hoped to be. A mature person examines himself, finds his faults, and gets to work on them. (PPL/49)

□   □   □

If you've been waiting until you are perfect to try to find God, come to Him today as an uncut and un-polished rock, just as you are, and He will come and bless you. (LFG/159)

□   □   □

As Christians we often want to improve our situa-tions but without too much effort on our part. We want spiritual victories the same way we want to lose weight without exercising or changing our lifestyle. But to free our minds from memories that bind takes work on our part. (FYM/69)

255

SELF-PITY

As children we express our displeasure with life by tears or tantrums. When we grow up we are proud that we have such self-control that we can keep all those negative emotions hidden. We do not cry when our friends plan a shopping trip without us—we are just deeply hurt. We do not slam down the receiver when our neighbor tells us she bought a new Lincoln; we just instruct our husband to start working overtime.

How easily we slip into the sin of self-pity instead of accepting the fact that God's plan for our life may not include a new Lincoln! (AEW/49)

SERVANTHOOD

One day Fred came home late and tired. Instead of commenting on his tardiness, I fixed him a cool drink, took it to our room, where he had collapsed in a chair, and knelt before him holding up the tray. He was so amazed and thrilled that he's never forgotten my one servile moment. While our knees may not often bend, our hearts should be seeking peace in our homes. (AEW/75)

SEXUALITY

Many unchurched people get their total opinion of Christianity from legalistic and unloving believers. They assume that the Christian life means giving up everything fun and retreating to a monastic existence. They are sure the Bible proclaims, "Frigidity is next to godliness."

Yet God created sex, and He approves of intimate relations within marriage. In 1 Corinthians 7:3-5 Paul instructs us that "The husband should give to his wife her conjugal rights, and likewise the wife to the husband." It is our loving duty. Does that sound like a God who wants us to be so sex-starved at home that we are ripe for roaming?

"And each should satisfy the other's needs." This phrase is preventive medicine. If each one of us satisfied the other's needs within marriage, we would have no reason to stray. What needs does your partner have that you are not meeting? So often when I talk with women whose husbands are unfaithful I ask, "What is that woman providing for him that you were unwilling to do?" (AEW/71)

Teenage Sexuality

God is not against sex; He invented it. But He intended it to be between two people who are committed to each other through marriage, two who are mature enough to be responsible parents. (OCP/73)

◻   ◻   ◻

With all the birth control devices and pills, with all the printed matter on the subject, there are still hundreds of thousands of teen-age pregnancies each year. There are still mistakes; things somehow go wrong. My sister-in-law once took in unwed mothers for the duration of their terms. Every one of them told her, "I never thought it would happen to me." (OCP/64)

□ □ □

What can be done with all these teenage pregnancies? The world says, "Have more classes on sex, provide free birth-control clinics, make abortions more easily available, expand Aid to Dependent Mothers." The solutions never seem to include teaching God's simple truth of reserving sex for marriage! We read nothing advising teens not to engage in sex—only articles on how to use contraceptives or how to abort an unwanted baby. (OCP/71)

SIN

When doubt and temptation get together they lead us quickly into sin. When Eve was convinced that God didn't mean what He had said, and that the fruit would make her wise, she took it and ate it. She used her own free will and disobeyed God's clear command that she knew so well. (AEW/57)

□ □ □

Not only can you trust God not to squeal on you, but you also can have confidence that He will rid you of your sin. In 1 John 5:14,15 we find: "And this is the confidence which we have before Him, that, if we ask anything according to His will, He hears us. And if we know that He hears us in whatever we ask, we know that we have the requests which we have asked from Him" (NAS).

When we are willing to ask in faith to be delivered of our sin, we can have confidence that He hears and acts.

I struggled with this scriptural concept at first because I could always find people who were so much worse than I was—Fred, for a close example. I never smoked, drank, or robbed banks. What more could God want from me? Yet one day I found a convicting verse: "For all have sinned and come short of the glory of God." Even Florence! (AEW/90-91)

□   □   □

One of the first things that happens to the new believer as he seeks fellowship with God is his overwhelming awareness of sin in his life. White lies (previously explainable acts), rebellious attitudes, loose morals, swearing, critical words, and other patterns of behavior that had appeared above average in the ways of the world, suddenly are seen as sin. (LFG/193)

STANDARDS

Because they have grown up in the ME generation, where morals are a thing of the past and where the only measure is "If it feels good, do it," young people see no need for old-fashioned standards. Where parents divorce easily and where television pictures as the norm beautiful people hopping daily from bed to bed, young people see no need for commitment. Yet they crave attention in this lonely world. Their desire to be loved by someone often leads them into romantic involvements so readily available. They don't count the possible cost. (OCP/53)

□   □   □

According to our own background, our spiritual beliefs, and our personality pattern, we develop what we consider a norm for ourselves. We have a feel for what's right and wrong, and people who don't see things our way become difficult. As we learn to deal with other people, we have to realize that just because they're different doesn't make them wrong, but it does make them harder to understand. (GAD/42-43)

SUBMISSION

The word *submission* has been so abused that no one wants to hear it mentioned. One pastor's wife informed us ahead of time that we were not to use the word *submission* at all in her church. Some feel that it means being a doormat, lying down on the floor to be stepped on. Some feel that it means suffering in silence for the glory of the Lord. Some feel that it means giving in to male superiority and worshiping chauvinism.

The actual meaning of submission is the absence of self-assertion, a willingness to yield versus resistance and rebellion. When we look at the word in its true significance we see why the Lord tells us to be submissive.

Submit yourselves to God (James 4:7). Start first by yielding to God.

Submit yourselves to your husbands (Ephesians 5:22). Be willing to please your husband, to put his needs before your own. Do not resist his suggestions and incite rebellion among the troops. Before I understood this principle I pretended to be submissive but was actually rebellious underneath. I rallied the children around good-fun mother and let them know that even though we obeyed Father when he was watching, we could live it up once he left town. Little did I realize what a terrible example of rebellion I was setting for my family! (AEW/99-100)

□ □ □

A submissive wife leads to a changed life for the whole family. (AEW/101)

SUICIDE

Carried to its extreme, the ultimate result of depression is suicide. In the June 1973 issue of *Psychology Today* we are told that approximately one out of 200 depressed persons commits suicide. (BBC/18)

□ □ □

A teenage girl in Arizona, depressed from her mother's remarriage because she felt left out and lonely, quickly went down the steps to despair. She became preoccupied with death and wrote an essay for her English class entitled "The Welcome at the Top of the Stairs." She developed the theory that in heaven she would get the recognition and love she felt she missed on earth. The teacher gave her an A, but did not recognize her plea for help. Later the girl's mother told how her daughter had smiled for the first time in months as she showed everyone her A. The family congratulated her, although no one took the time to read the essay. Two days later her mother went in to wake her and found her dead. Beside her was an empty bottle of sleeping pills and in her hand the essay with the A. It is important to realize that *a sudden improvement after a long period of depression may mean the end is near.* (BBC/30-31)

T

TALKING

When we stop talking and start loving, we give God a chance. (AEW/101)

□   □   □

There was never much "inner" about my personality. As the expression goes, I let it all hang out, but as I studied the Bible I saw the necessity of a gentle spirit for the first time. I was not to be bossy and controlling but loving and gentle. I was not to be the loud life-of-the-party but the quiet support of my husband. Fred once said to me, "When you talk all the time you don't learn anything, for you already know what you're saying." (AEW/102)

TELEVISION

So much of our perspective on people in the news comes through television that we often think of real life activities as media events. We begin to assume the White House is a painted backdrop created for the nightly news, that the First Ladies' ball gowns came out of some costume rental company, and that political campaigns have been cast with actors capable of pulling high ratings. As theatrical productions, presidential campaigns fill in the gaps between seasons of baseball and football and provide relief from crime and violence. (PPO/13)

□   □   □

We have all read facts about the children of today being more out of shape than any previous generation. Most of them come home from school and head straight for the refrigerator and then the TV. They eat snacks with high calories and low nourishment and avoid exercise, both physical and mental, while watching TV.

Following the suggestions of doing homework first and balancing TV with reading will help cut down on television time, but the underlying message that must be presented is that TV watching is a last resort. Other activities need to be offered to fill the time that would be spent in front of the TV. Find a sports event of interest to your children and sign them up for a team. [Outdoor activities] help build team spirit, physical health, and they are not done in front of a TV.

If your child is not athletically inclined or if after sports still has too much time on his or her hands, offer lessons such as piano, violin, art, or dance. Most of the YM- or YWCAs across the country offer many options for such activities at a very reasonable cost. Another choice might be to enroll your older children in a reading program at the local library where they receive points and prizes for the number of books read. Be alert; there are many options available that put your children's mental and physical growth first and make TV a last choice. (RTC/121)

TEMPERAMENTS

Four hundred years before Christ was born, Hippocrates first presented the concept of the temperaments to the world. As a physician and philosopher, he dealt closely with people and saw that there were extroverts and introverts, optimists and pessimists. He further categorized people according to their body fluids as Sanguine, blood; Choleric, yellow bile; Melancholy, black bile; and Phlegmatic, phlegm. While modern psychologists do not hold to the theory of the fluids, the terms and characteristics are still valid. (AEW/22).

□   □   □

In these times of global tension and inner turmoil, I find so many Christian people who are longing for some sense of identity and self-worth, some answers to their frustrations and searchings. They study the Word; they know they are created in God's image and made slightly lower than the angels; they've been crucified in Christ and have taken off the old clothes and put on the new. They've gone to church, knelt at the altar on Sunday, and taught Bible studies. In spite of all these positive spiritual steps, they still need some simple solution to who they really are as individuals.

After these twenty years of studying and teaching the temperaments, I am still amazed at how God uses this tool to open people's eyes to themselves and their relationships with others. (YPT/34)

□   □   □

The Popular wants the FUN WAY.

The Powerful wants MY WAY.

The Perfect wants the RIGHT WAY.

The Peaceful wants the EASY WAY. (PPO/31)

□   □   □

The Populars were voted most likely to succeed.

The Perfects were depressed for fear they wouldn't succeed.

The Peacefuls didn't care whether they would or wouldn't succeed.

The Powerfuls passed them all by and succeeded. (PPO/22)

□   □   □

The SANGUINE wants attention and credit.

The MELANCHOLY wants order and discipline.

The CHOLERIC wants action and obedience.

The PHLEGMATIC wants peace and quiet. (GAD/38)

□   □   □

As I teach the concept of the temperaments in *Personality Plus* seminars, people sometimes ask me, "Are you trying to put us into little boxes?" As I have given this question much thought, I have come to the realization that we are already in our own little boxes. As we come to any experience in life, we bring our own structure along; we go only as far as we are comfortable. We don't climb over our portable walls and peek through the cracks before opening the gate.

When we are first born, we are instantly put in our own little box. We are walled into our tiny space and wheeled over to a window, where fond relatives can look down into our box and view our helpless forms. We're wrapped into a tight bundle to be brought home and placed into our new box, a crib with bars around for our protection. For outings we are placed in a basket or strapped in an infant seat—even in the supermarket we're put inside a shopping cart for security. As we move up to bigger boxes, we're installed in a playpen, which keeps us in our place, and later, we're allowed to roam our room with a gate across the doorway. As we get daring, we're given the freedom of a fenced-in backyard. Each school grade has its room, and we settle in for a year, nestled in a protected space with a teacher.

We grow up in boxes, and even as we get out into the big world, we bring our walls along. When I had my first college roommate we were both put into one box, but within days we had put up an invisible wall between us. We couldn't agree on bedspreads, wall posters, or housekeeping, so we put a strip of masking tape across the tile floor, and we each took our half of the room, turned our backs on each other, and created our own boxes where we felt secure.

The concept of the temperaments doesn't fence us in and put our feet in cement, but it does help us to see what kind of a box we're in, and how to move out of it. As we realize how imprisoned we are by our basic weaknesses, we can work to open the gate and dare to stray over to the yard next door. As we understand our differences, we have more tolerance for a person who wants to live in a style contrary to our desires. (PPL/146-147)

□   □   □

The knowledge of the temperaments can help each one of us to function better in social situations; to converse in a manner which will be appropriate and pleasing to the others present; and to understand the positives and the negatives of other people. (PPL/166)

THANKFULNESS

Those of us who are parents are always thrilled when our children appreciate us, when they say thanks.

Several times during Marita's teens when she fussed because we wouldn't let her do a certain thing, she returned later to say, "Thank you for saying no." In the same way our Father loves to hear thanks from His children even when we are not enthused over our circumstances. We're here for a reason and only our Father can weave together our past, our present, and our future. (AEW/95-96)

THINKING

It doesn't take much to think ABOVE AVERAGE because the average person doesn't think much. Henry James, the turn-of-the-century psychologist, said that the average person uses only 10 percent of his available brain power. Do you see how little extra you would have to think to be ABOVE AVERAGE? If you exerted only 2 percent beyond your norm, you'd be on your way; if you doubled your thinking capacity, you'd be close to brilliant! (ITS/49)

□   □   □

As I began to teach those in the seminars to think on four tracks, we developed an acrostic to help us remember how to communicate more effectively:

Material

Organization

Response

Emotion

As Christians we need to be able to think MORE than we've been used to doing. You may not have checked your mind recently to find out what its potentials are but start stretching and training a four-track mind. (ITS/57)

□   □   □

As we begin to realize how little time we spend in solitary meditation, is it any wonder our brain is only functioning at one-tenth of its potential? If you wish to speed up your thinking process, start by finding a "think spot" and setting aside time to use it. Once you find how much fun it is to expand your creative ability, you will see "think spots" everywhere: in your car, in line at the supermarket, in the dentist's waiting room, in church. Make use of them, think constantly. (ITS/60)

269

If you want to increase your mental ability, start with the past. Don't be too busy with the present to reflect on the lessons of the past. (ITS/66)

TRAINING

How many of us refuse to do what God wants us to do because we don't have the proper training! My husband and I began teaching Bible studies before we had studied the Bible. We knew that this was what God wanted us to do. If we had waited until we felt sufficiently trained, we would not have started yet. God knew what He was doing with us. In having to teach we had to study, and the majority of our Christian growth has come from the preparation we have had to do to keep ahead of a class. When God calls us to do a job, we should never answer that we are not prepared; we should just get to work. He will give us the power of performance! (AEW/44)

U

UNIQUENESS

Although we can't make other people choose us as special, we have the power to give others the unique feeling of being special. What a gift we bestow—far better than a new doll—when we pin the label SPECIAL on a child, on a note, on a friend, on a lonely elder.

We all want to be that chosen person; we want to be loved. So many sad and lonely people I talk to are waiting for someone to find them, to make them special; yet the best way to find this unique relationship is to give it away to someone else. (OCP/43)

□　　□　　□

Why does a businessman pour his whole life out to some young thing he met at the water cooler? Because he doesn't think his wife really cares—and she may not. He's not attracted to this girl for her beauty or brains, but because she sensed he had a need to share his needs, and she was available to listen. I've had wives ask me, "What can he see in her? She's plain and simpleminded and hasn't got half my talent. What has she got that I don't have?"

It isn't *what she's got*, it's *how she makes him feel*. She seems to understand his needs. (OCP/44)

271

W

WEALTH

Some of us feel that it is a lack of money that holds us down. Gideon replied to God's request, "O my Lord, wherewith shall I save Israel? Behold, my family is poor in Manasseh, and I am *the least* in my father's house" (Judges 6:15). With no finances behind him at all, Gideon was turned into a wise prophet by God's commanding power. Many times I have had sweet Christians tell me they cannot have friends in for fellowship because they do not have good china or matching napkins, because their house is too small, or because their talent is too slight. But these are only excuses for our unwillingness to do as God has asked us. "Open your homes to each other without complaining" (1 Peter 4:9, TEV). I would enjoy a peanut butter sandwich if someone else prepared it and handed it to me.

The world tells us that we need money to be happy, but, as God told Gideon, "Surely I will be with thee." Should not His presence be assurance enough? (AEW/44-45)

WEDDINGS

My high school speech and drama pupils all loved weddings as much as I did, and they volunteered to help

272

stage the production [of my own wedding]. This would be no Tom Thumb wedding, but a coronation with me as the queen. Four of my leading ladies were to be bridesmaids in yellow gowns, and every girl who had a strapless fluffy-net evening dress and was willing to show up at the wedding became part of the court. My college roommate, Hazel, was chosen maid-of-honor and was draped in aqua silk. I found twins with Shirley Temple curls for flower girls and an adorable little boy for the ring bearer in rented tails.

Every Monday after school we had committee meetings on the high-school stage for those anxious to participate, and their creative ideas caught up with mine. The girls planned the royal buffet, the home ec teacher made my crown, the woodshop boys made scepters out of broomsticks, the metal shop built display racks for the gifts, the autoshop boys found me a long white Cadillac, and the high school band began practicing the wedding march.

Wedding fever swept the high school as Cinderella got ready to meet Prince Charming at the altar and live happily ever after. As a creative writing project one of my pupils summed up the excitement of the entire student body in a letter to *Life* magazine, and the editor caught the youthful spirit right off the paper. Since they were already looking for a bride for a bride-of-the-year, *Life* thought my wedding offered a new twist and they decided to hurry up to Haverhill.

To have *Life* come to my wedding was beyond even my exaggerated dreams, and my royal court was ecstatic. Imagine, Miss Chapman and her followers spread across the pages of the most popular magazine in the country! We held emergency meetings to intensify our efforts and dramatize the details.

For the two weeks before the wedding my every move was photographed, and I lay awake at night creating clever ad libs for the next day and practicing how to look surprised at a shower I had planned for myself. My brother Ron, now the top show-biz personality in Dallas, swept ahead of me as I made entrances and he kept everyone laughing in the role of court jester. We were on stage from the moment we got up each day, and we both loved it.

By the night of the wedding everyone in Haverhill knew that Miss Chapman was getting married. Young men in tuxedos helped me in and out of the long white Cadillac, and the police blocked off the entire square with long white horses usually reserved to hold back crowds at parades. There *were* crowds and this was *more* than a parade.

I walked the length of the church driveway through the rows of cheering students, my crowned head held high as I had seen the new Queen Elizabeth do at her recent coronation.Temporary floodlights were beaming on me from the church rafters, and my college music professor was playing the organ with all the stops pulled out. As he hit those chilling notes preceding "Here Comes the Bride," the audience arose in unison and turned their heads in my direction, and I marched down the aisle on my brother Jim's arm as the twins threw rose petals in my path.

It was a perfect night: the wedding of two perfect people in a perfect setting. *But* — after every wedding comes a marriage. (AEW/9-11).

WEIGHT

So many women come to me with weight problems that have become such burdens to them that the concerns are usurping control over their actions and personalities. Some have supposedly tried every diet in the world and can't lose an ounce. They've bought every diet book and gone to every health seminar and nothing has helped. I know one girl who has three lifetime memberships in health clubs and only has "guilt over not going" as her result. Many women talk endlessly about their diets and defeats, making themselves not only overweight but boring.

What do you do if you can't overcome a problem and you have sincerely tried? You accept the situation and say, "Dear Lord, You know I don't want to be this way. I have tried to eliminate this area of my life and it's still here. Help me to accept myself as I am and not ruin my whole life over one problem. I know You made me and love me and don't want me harping on this subject any longer. When You are ready, lead me to victory." (ITS/28)

WIVES

There is little hope for us to have happy husbands when we are belligerent and domineering. When we preach liberation and are trying to find ourselves, it is impossible to have our men want to be the kind of sweet Christians that we are. Yet when we aim to please, our husbands see a spirit in us that is hard to resist. We can win them over by our conduct. We won't have to say a word. (AEW/100)

□   □   □

It is impossible to love our husbands until we love the Lord. When we can communicate on a personal level with the Lord, we can hope to be in tune with our husbands. *Redbook* magazine, in one of its many surveys, proclaimed on the cover "Religious Women Make Better Lovers." While they couldn't put their finger on the reason, they had to conclude that those women surveyed who had a "strong faith" were more happily married. When we start each day talking quietly with the Lord, we're less apt to scream at our husbands. When we keep our eyes looking up instead of around, we're not going to keep a record of wrongs. When we're able to see our husband's inner self, we're not so concerned with physique. When we do all things heartily as unto the Lord (Colossians 3:23), we consider housework an investment in marriage. (AEW/98)

□   □   □

Why are religious women better lovers? Because they love the Lord, have submissive attitudes toward their husbands, and are aiming for quiet, gentle spirits that are of great value in the sight of God and man. (AEW/103)

□   □   □

We women have the beautiful opportunity of bringing love into our homes. What we show our families reflects in their behavior. When your husband and children leave in the morning and you smile, kiss them, and say, "I love you," you set the tone for their day. How many of us give trouble instead of love!

"Don't drive too fast and kill yourself, you dummy. The insurance isn't paid."

"Are you wearing that horrible shirt to school again?"

"Don't bring home any more of your stupid friends."

What is the last thing you give your family each morning?

Not all of us are natural beauty queens, but we should do the best we can with what we have. Fred says that if you could see the real me, you would know that I have done more than could be expected with the raw material available. While God looks on our hearts, humans see us on the surface, and we should make the view as pleasant as possible.

One very chubby lady told me she didn't think it was important how she looked, because if her husband were really spiritual he would see the beauty underneath. I wasn't sure the Lord Himself could have gotten through that 250 pounds to the beauty underneath! (AEW/74)

◻   ◻   ◻

When I go to K mart, my people-watching store, I am often amazed at what I see walking down the aisle. Here strolls a sloppy young thing in terrycloth shorts with her fat legs jiggling as she moves. Her bosoms hang out of her skimpy midriff as she leans over to keep the baby from falling out of the basket. Her head is strewn with pink rollers, and a lime-green net bonnet is tied under her chins.

I look at a woman like that and say to myself, "That was once a bride." But no man ever married that. There's no way any man with any degree of sense would have stood at the altar and watched that walk down an aisle. He married a princess and she turned into a frog. (AEW/74)

WOMEN

We women want so much to be loved. We want our man to put his arms around us, to comfort us, to speak kindly to us, to care for us. If we know you love us, we can put up with other discomforts, but if we're not sure, we'll ask for the moon to test you. (AEW/115)

◻   ◻   ◻

Men, do you see a pattern here?

When you criticize us, we get worse.

When you compliment us, we get better.

When you try to change us, we won't budge.

When you accept us as we are, we try to improve.

When you don't help us, we're mad because you're sitting.

When you're willing to assist, we insist that you sit down.

When you pick on the children, we think you hate us.

When you are positive and encouraging, we know you love us.

When you are too busy to listen, we nag and ramble.

When you set aside time to converse, we condense our comments.

We're really so easy to please when you love us. You can turn our whole lives around when you let us know we come first. (AEW/138)

WORDS

While presenting a children's sermon, I explained that when our words come out of our mouths they should be like little presents all wrapped up to be given away. The idea of presents brightened the children up and one precious little picture-book girl stood up, stepped into the aisle and said loudly to the whole congregation (as if serving as my interpreter), "What she means is that our words should be like little silver boxes with bows on top."

As the adults nodded and murmured affirmations, I exclaimed, "What a beautiful thought! Our words should be gifts to each other, little silver boxes with bows on top." (BOX)

□　　□　　□

As we think about giving out kind words, silver boxes, in place of expensive presents, we would probably agree with Ralph Waldo Emerson when he said, "Rings and jewels are not gifts, but apologies for gifts. The only gift is a portion of thyself." Somehow in our materialistic society we have come to equate giving with money and possessions that can be held in our hands. But when we reflect on the turning points in our lives, we often find they came at the encouragement of a person who believed in us, a person who took the time and perhaps the risk to give a portion of himself to someone in need. (BOX)

□   □   □

How simple it sounds to say only those words which will edify and build up the listener. How we would like each one of our words to minister grace or do a favor for the hearer. One day I was attending a church service and was asked on the spot to give a children's sermon. I stood before rows of young people and taught them Ephesians 4:29 from memory. As I broke it into parts, I asked, "What does it mean to 'minister grace'?"

A boy accurately stated, "Do a favor."

"What else?" I asked and a little girl said, "It's like giving someone a present full of words."

I loved her simple concept and asked the children to think of their conversation as opportunities to give presents to their friends.

How about you? Are your words presents? When you speak to your child, your parent, your mate, do you do them a favor? (ITS/32)

□   □   □

The beauty of the written word is that it can be held close to the heart and read over and over again. An oral silver box may tarnish with the passage of time and the trials of life, but one that is written can be taken out and read and reread. With each reading the glow is enhanced like the finish on fine sterling—it gets more beautiful with each polishing. (BOX)

□   □   □

We don't stop to realize the harm we can do with our words. But as we have reviewed how others have hurt our self-image in the past, we want to be careful that we aren't doing the same thing. I have learned from available statistics that we tend to repeat the mistakes of our parents. For example, a boy who was beaten by his father, hated every minute of mistreatment and vowed he'd never lay a hand on his son, grew up to beat his child. Our intellect tells us not to do these negative things, but when we are in a stressful situation, we react emotionally as our parents did in the same set of circumstances. We don't map out our feelings, we just react instantly. (ITS/33)

□   □   □

How many well-meaning Christians have written someone off in a moment of poor judgment and lived to regret it? How many grandmothers can't enjoy their grandchildren because they "wrote off" their daughter for some grievous sin and have never been willing to humble themselves and restore fellowship? Oh dear friends, don't lash out with words you'll have to eat later and if you already have, eat them quickly and restore "the years that the locusts hath eaten . . . " (Joel 3:25). (ITS/160)

□   □   □

281

When we are in control of our senses, we can stop damaging words before they get out. Some of us Sanguines get our mouth in motion before our brain is in gear, and we live to regret it. We must train ourselves to think before we speak. Once the words are out, we can't stuff them back in; they are intangible, illusive.

On Marita's fourth birthday she received four talcum powder mitts. No child needed that much powder, so I put them away. The following Sunday we had company, and while the adults lingered over dessert the children went to Marita's room to play. After a while a little girl came out ghostly white from head to toe. Only her eyes stood out. The mothers all ran to see what had happened. The children had found the four talcum mitts and they had powdered each other completely. Every particle of powder was out of the mitts and the room was a mist of white. For months when we walked on Marita's carpet little puffs of powder appeared.

Many families have done the same with words. We've covered each other with angry barbs and sarcastic accusations. We've hit each other with demeaning phrases and we can't get them back. No matter how we try to apologize, those words are out there floating loose. We can't stuff them back in our mitts, and when we tread on certain subjects those words come up as dust between our toes. (AEW/188)

WORK CHARTS

I have found from my own experience and from talking to teens that they don't mind doing some work if they know ahead of time and don't get surprised at the last minute. Our Family Work Chart had the children's names and also Fred and I were listed. We wanted to make sure that the children didn't think this was a slave labor camp but a division of responsibility. If I noticed something broken, I would write it in Fred's column and if the children had a need they could write a request in mine. The children rarely did this but they had permission to ask for our help. (RTC/125)

□　　□　　□

At one point a newspaper reporter came to our home to interview me on our "Harmony in the Home" class. I knew Freddie would come home while she was there and I thought of warning him to be sure and behave well. Then I realized he might walk in and say something like "Are you the lady I'm supposed to behave for?" I decided that I'd trained him enough and I'd take my chances.

When he came home from fifth grade that day, he walked into the family room and I introduced him to the reporter. He greeted her pleasantly, left the room, and returned within a few minutes holding a dry mop, a dish towel, a rubber band, and a can of Endust. The reporter asked him what he was going to do and he answered her as if I'd rehearsed him. "Each day when I come home from school I check the work chart to see what I am expected to do. Today I'm to mop the foyer floor so I have my mop which I will cover with this clean towel held on by this rubber band. I will spray the towel with Endust and then mop up the floor."

The reporter was amazed and said, "I never saw a child before who did his chores without anyone having to remind him."

283

I can guarantee that if you organize your household responsibilities and put up a chart each Thursday your children will keep cleaning cheerfully, but I can assume that if you don't come up with some form of disciplined duties, your children won't devise it on their own.

Remember that training up each child in the way he should go is not just to make your work load easier, but to prepare him to become a responsible adult who will be able to get along without you. (RTC/126)

WORSHIP

If we wish to know God personally, we must first establish Him as the only object worthy of worship and fall down before Him in a spirit of reverence. (LFG/149)

□   □   □

When we put our focus on any activity, person, thing, or compulsion to such a degree that we are worshiping it, being mentally consumed by it, we are bowing before something other than God. (LFG/150)

□   □   □

Because God created the world in six days and then rested on the seventh, He commands us to do the same. Work is a necessity of life, but God wants us to rest from our pursuits one day a week and worship Him. (LFG/150)

Index

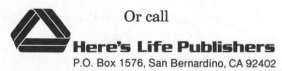